Assam
Xunor Xophura
The Golden Valley

Sumanta Barooah

Sumanta Barooah
Assam *'Xunor Xophura'* The Golden Valley

First Published: 2010

Design & Layout
Shadow Concepts
New Delhi

Published By
Loyang Publishing
Jervois Road
Singapore

@ Sumanta Barooah 2010

Printed & Bound In India

'To know the origins is initiation into the Tao'
-LaoTzu

This book is dedicated to my family
Sushil Borooah,Usha,Lalita,Shawna,Rubina
Pavan,Prithvi and Manav.

assam,the Golden Valley

Acknowledgement

It is fabled that people, in their quest, travel all over the world and only return to discover one's own neighborhood. And so I did. Over the years the distant lands, once a mention or a chapter in my Geography classes became land marks, with a memory, a picture, a cultural discovery and in many occasions a source of joy and inspiration. Travel is such a large canvas, it is always refreshing to rediscover the countries, the haunts, the landmarks, yet the people , the culture, the cuisine remain the same possibly re-presented in the vogue of the day.

I am from the NorthEast born and brought up at a time when travel was adverturous and places were unified and simple. The means of transportation was cumbersome, but the journeys 'simply' awesome.

My cousins, friends and some travelling companions urged me to do this book some years ago, but every time I sat down to complete it my thoughts would wander off to places in Arunachal or Manipur or Nagaland or Meghalaya, where I grew up, schooling. No journey in the North East can be complete unless one transgress two or three Political States of the present "Seven Sisters" I personally felt that all that has changed is, we have multiple sets of politicians, governments, cars, regulations and egos being paid for by the same simple people who have lived peacefully for centuries and continue to do so today.

This a pictorial essay of some of the important landmarks of Assam assimilated on the format of various travel books and brochures I have seen the world over, to be used as a travel planner or a travel companion and it is not even close to being a travel Bible. These are only memorable pictures of a beautiful land to give you the perspective of Assam which you cannot fathom in the postage stamp pictures of the internet.

I must thank, Dilip Tamuli, Rajiv Bora, Surajit Jaradhara friends and family who accompanied me on these picture excursions, Mr.Kamal Goswami of the Assam Tourism Development Corporation, who earnestly felt the need for such a book, Ms. Deepa Laskar, who egged me on to discover the nooks and corners, Mr. Absar Hazarika and Mr. Swapnanil Barooah who have unmitigated love for the Golden Valley of the Brahmaputra, Assam.
And Mr. Manoj Das the Assamese 'Gaobura' of Delhi.

Contents

Acknowledgement	VI
Contents	VIII
Arrivals	X
The Golden Valley	2
Brahmaputra	6
Tourism Map of Assam	8
Assamese Jewellery	10
Assamese Cuisine	12
Sui Ka Pha	14
Sibsagar	16
The Ahom Kingdom	18
Charaideo	26
Sri Sri Shankardev	28
Borduwa	30
Majuli	34
Borpeta	44
Guwahati	54
Madan Kamdev	62
Orang	65
Pobitara	66

Hajo	68
Pua Mecca	72
Manas Tiger Reserve	74
Surya Pahar	78
Eco Camp, Nameri	84
Bhalukpong	88
Tezpur	90
Malinithan	94
Kaziranga Sanctuary	96
Dhekia Khowa Satra	102
Dibrugarh	104
Buddhist Monuments	106
Haflong, Karbi Hills	108
Jatinga	110
Silchar	112
Digboi	113
Ledo, the last station	114
Wildlife Parks & Sanctuaries	116
Festivals of Assam	126
Ethnic people of Assam	134
Brief History of Assam	178
Colonial Assam	184
Ancient Monuments in Assam	186

MongMao

assam,the Golden Valley

Arrivals

Many fables exist in the folklores of China, Myanmar, and other neighbors to our east, describing a river valley in the west where the rice grains grow in plentiful and are as golden, as the magic metal.

The Tsangpo~Siang~Brahmaputra~Jamuna valley is generous along the Assam Valley, where at harvest time you see horizons of the shimmering golden grain.
Even Sukhapa, the prince from Mong Mao, a kingdom bordering Burma with the province of Yunnan in China, came looking for his **'Xunor Xophura'** the golden casket, traversing the journey through the dense forests of the Eastern Himalayas and the Patkai Hills with his entourage of 9000 over a period of 13 years to arrive and settle here.

In fact it is estimated that 11 influxes have taken place over the centuries to the valley, making it probably the only place in the world to have a conglomerate society of Mon-Khamer, Astro-Asiatic, Tibeto-Burman and Indo Aryan living peacefully, intermingling culture, religion, rituals, graces and cuisine.

People came from Tibet via BumLa, TseLa, and Tunga passes, across the Patkai Hills via Diphu, Kumjawng, Hpungan, Chokham, Pangsau and More-Tamu, from Myanmar across Arakan Yoma by Via An and Taungup.

Possibly the earliest migration was of the Mon-Khamer speakers today identified as Khasi and Synteng who came from South East Asia. They were followed by the Tibeto-Burman group of the Eastern Himalayas. The third group was the Indo-Aryans after 500B.C. from North India and the Gangetic Valley. This migration continued until about 1205 when the first Muslims arrived. These were the captive soldiers of the Bakhtiar Khilji army. They were followed by Sukhapa in 1228, who arrived via the Pangsau pass from Mong Mao with his Ahom army. The Ahoms were followed by the Buddhists, Khamti, Khamyang, Aiton, Phake and Turung who were of the same ethnicity as the Ahoms.

Colonial period brought about uncertainty to the whole Brahmaputra delta when Kachin and KukiChin people ingressed via the Patkai and the Arkan Yoma. The development of the Tea Industry brought about the Mundari speaking, migration from Central India.

Illustrated herein is the realtime **Golden Valley**..

assam, the Golden Valley

assam, the Golden Valley

The Golden Valley

The caressing rays of the October sun flowing into the shadows of the ever-so-green trees accentuating the never-ending horizon of the golden harvest, the cloudless skies of autumn alight with the golden glow, the moment stood still. This is my home, the Golden Valley.

Emotions overcome my sensibility, urging me to hold-on to the moment, eternally, I take a moment to thank God, I thank the being within me, created on the love and trudge of my family to be part of this wonderful land. I am happy to be me; and this is my identity.

There is beauty in nature, wherever you seek, there is empathy, there is compassion, there is truth, wherever you quest. Yet the smells, the sounds, the silence here, pulls my heart-strings, generating a euphoric light-headedness, a sense of belonging. But then, this is my land.

Possibly, this Golden Valley is the only place in the world where people from five ethnic backgrounds have lived together for centuries, peacefully, intermingling languages, culture, cuisine and lifestyles. People from distances even as far as China heard of this valley of rice and came to discover the land and made it their home; possibly, the empathy of the Rice-Culture, unified all who came to this Brahmaputra Valley. At this very moment it is being debated, whether Assam is where the Golden Grain originated from.

Political priorities of today have divided the area into seven states, yet the neighbors among themselves refer to the region as the unified land of the **Seven Sisters.**

As a wise man wrote, " rivers crystallize civilizations and allow the transmission of the cultures inside the continents. Relief, mountains, plains, valleys delimit the territories naturally…But the territories are made to pass from one's to another one's hands.. History is the spectacle of these crystallizations and exchanges (not always peaceful), seen through a deformed vision which is the political territories superimposing on the natural territories "

Assam reveres the mighty Brahmaputra all along the valley as it journeys to the sea. It is the heart and the soul of the people lured here from distant lands to cultivate its fertile banks.The other important valley of the state is that of the Barak. Both these rivers shed into the Bay of Bengal after a short journey through Bangladesh.

The golden valley of the Brahmaputra harbored centuries of migration from all directions, settling them in the vast expanse of its alluvial river banks. People came looking for the wonder grain 'rice' and a conglomerate culture evolved. But, it was only with the arrival of the *Ahom King Sukhapa* that it started taking the shape of a country/ state/Kingdom, as a whole, in the 13th century.
However its indigenous cultural identity had to wait another 300 years until the birth of the Saint *Srimanta Sankerdev*, to inculcate and establish it's religion, philosophy and graces, the very essence of the Assamese culture. Today, considered as one of the politest culture of the world.

Predominantly, a Hindu religion and culture dominated society with strong indigenous graces, rituals, practices, dance, dramas, and philosophy preached by this 16th century saint/philosopher *Srimanta Shankardeo*;. Essentially *neo-Viashnuism*, it was called '*Mahapurushia Dharma*' It was propagated in a local folklore, poems, hymns, dance, drama routine conceived, written and enacted under *Sri Sri Shankardeo* 's tutelage. This formes the quintessence of the Assamese society yesterday and today. Living example of his philosophy and practice is still prevalent in the *Satras* of Majuli island, notably the *Dakhinpath Satra*.
This is a pictorial essay of the Golden Valley. A book is never complete unlike a painting. It is a picture conceived and transcribed from a point of view. It is forever moving, ever changing as is the dynamism of life.
As rightly enunciated in an Assamese proverb '*Samayer Tikoni Aag phale*', Time has a tail in front not behind, one can never catch up.

No matter where you seek, you may not find God, but should you come to Assam, I assure you, you will come very close to doing so.
The local history till the arrival of the Mon Kings is disjointed and probably being researched somewhere abroad. Sometimes I wonder why indigenous history is always researched in foreign lands.
Archeological finds all over the valley relate to periods of Ancient Indian history. Folklores and stories abound, built around the main Indian Epics.
Continuous written history starts only with the arrival of Sukhapa from the East, more precisely Mong Mau, in the present Province of Yunnan in China near the famous town of Ruilli.

A dynastic rule followed that lasted close to six hundred years, until the annexation by the British. A short period of war torn administration by the Burmese kings preceded the British administration.

The Assam Valley and some of its historical towns are often mentioned in the Indian Epics and have quite often found mention in history as part of some of the greater kingdoms of the Indian subcontinent.

I being neither a historian or a social scientist would like to bring to you a real-time impression of the state, its people and its culture as I believe the identity Assamese was constructed by the great Ahom king *Sukhapa* Chaolung and the build as a culture by the saint *Srimanta Shankardev*.

The gateway to the North East has always been Guwahati, the old kingdom of Kamarupa. Actually the river Brahmaputra, bifurcates the state along the whole valleyand the banks are referred to as the North-bank and the South-bank. For some unearthly reason the South-bank towns have fared better than their complimentary towns, possibly the shadow of the Chinese invasion in 1962 into the North-bank and better prospects of trade with Bangladesh, Myanmar, Thailand for the South-bankers.

Similarly,by some colonial logic it is also divided into Upper Assam and Lower Assam. Although the central districts are nor popularly called central Assam, the Districts to the East are called Upper Assam and the districts west of Guwahati are generally called Lower Assam. The North Bank, as per today's demarcations extends a little beyond the riverbank itself and the districts thereof. The North Bank Hills are today's Arunachal Pradesh.The South Bank is deeper and includes Karbi Along and the Barak Valley, which has Silchar as a focal point of development on the border of Bangladesh

As one travels in the area one can hardly differentiate the district or the state borders.The ethnic demarcation is so many and so frequent, largely diffrentiated by peoples attire and their celebrations but never due to the politically enforced boundaries.
In this photo-essay we bring to you a glimpse of Assam of today with a brief background of the people and their culture, the history and the hidden destinations of a state yet tobe discovered.
A countryside and a culture which is ever so hospitable; where the neighbourhood has a name and not just a number.

assam, the Golden Valley

Brahmaputra

The Brahmaputra Starts fom the Jima Yangzong Glacier near mount Kailash in the Northern Himalayas.Known in China s the Yarlung Tsangpo it is the highest of the major rivers in the world.

It flows for about 1700 Kilometers west at a height of 4000 Meters upto Mt Namcha Barwa and turns southwards at the Yarlung Tsangponear Canyon , till now called the Great Bend. This is considered the Highest Canyon in the World.

It enters India near the town of and is called Siang. In its journey of the next 100 Kilometers it descends from its over 700 feet to almost the sea level at Pasighat where it is also called the Dihang till it meets the Lohit and the Dibang rivers to makeup the Brahmaputra.

All along its journey through Assam it is called the Brahmaputra, the son of Brahma, with some stretches as wide as 10 Kilometers to almost a kilometer width as it cuts through the rocks of the Shillong plateau.This is where the famous battle of Saraighat was fought and the moghuls were defeated repeatedly. As it traverses through the plains of Assam ,near the town of Dibrugarh and the Lakhimpur district it bifurcates into two channels and then further down about a 100 Kilometers meets again, forming the famous island of Majuli in between.

Crossing the towns of Guwahati, Hajo, Goalpara and Dhubri it moves into Bangladesh where it is called the Jamuna,further on it meets the Ganga and as an amlgamated river called the Padma reaches out to the Bay of Bengal,. On its final run it meets the Barak river which in Bangladesh is clled the Meghna.This is one of the largest delta system in the world.

Courtesy Assam Tourism Development Corporation

assam, the Golden Valley

Traditional Assamese Jewellery

Dugdugi

Kerumoni

Thuriya

GaamKharu

Muthi

Courtesy:'Majuli Ek Saanj",Guwahati

assam,the Golden Valley

Basic Assamese Cuisine

Khar
Pitika
Pura/Bhaja

Bhat
Dali
Masor Anja
Mangsho
Masor Tenga

Payokh
Mitha

Siu Ka Pha Chaolung
The King who gave Assam an identity
1191-1268.C

Many legends exist about Siu-Ka-Pha, *ChaoLung* (meaning The Great). Simply put, he was a Prince from Mong Mao, a state on the border of Myanmar and the Chinese province of Yunnan near the present day town of Ruilli. Born in 1191to ChaoChang-ngyeo, a direct descendant of Khun-lung, the legendary king and Nang Mong Blok Kham Seng.

As the King, his uncle did not have a son he was nominated the crown prince of Mong Mao. However, a scion born at a later stage to the queen, usurped his throne. During this period both Sukhapa's father and uncle died in his home state, but rather than going back home, he decided to travel west to conquer and establish his own kingdom. He ventured west looking for his bowl of gold the *'Xunor Xophura'*.

Sukhapa left KingSen MaoLung, the capital of Mong Mao in 1215. He was accompanied by his three queens, two sons, several nobles and their families, soldiers totaling more than nine thousand peole. He also took with him two elephants and three hundred Yunnanese pack mules. They followed an ancient route that passed through Myitkyiena, Mogaung, Hukwang in the upper Irrawaddy basin to reach the Patkai hill in 1227.An arduous journey of over 12 years.

In the Patkai hills he founded a province called Khamjang where he placed a governor called Thaomong Khamjang. Kham-jang henceforth became the eastern boundary of the Ahom kingdom.

He crossed the Patkai hills at Namrup and came to the Upper Buri-Dihing region on the 2nd of December 1228, where he founded another province and placed a governor. Henceforth 2nd of December is commemorated as Assam Diwas, the day Sukhapa set foot in Assam.

He looked high and lo for his 'Xunor Xophura' the bowl of gold in the coming years, finally arriving at Charaideo where he found the soil most suitable for habitation and wet-rice cultivation.

assam,the Golden Valley

This is where he established his capital in 1253. Charaideo is called Che-rai-doi or Che-tam-doi, or Che Kham-run. Sukhapa finally sent messengers to Mon Mao from here with presents to the Mao King informing his safe arrival in Mong Pa-kam. He remained there till his death in 1268 A.D.

Charaideo thus became the capital of the new Ahom kingdom and remained so for the next 145 years. Initially, Siu-ka-pha's kingdom was bounded by the Brahmaputra, the Buri-Dihing, the Dikhow, rivers on the three sides and the Naga Hills on the south. This very Kingdom eventually expanded to cover whole Brahmaputra valley. The Tai's had brought their own historians along with them and all matters of the state were recorded in local gazettes called *Burunjis*.

An able administrator he encouraged the invaders to marry local women and intermingle with the existing culture. He subjugated the local chiefs and kings to form a unified Kingdom. The people called the invaders Ha –Cham which eventually became Assam and the people were referred to as Tai-Ahoms. The Ahoms ruled Assam for the next 600 years until the conflicts with the Burmese Kings and the advent of the British.

Sukhapa of Mong Mao gave the valley its own individual identity, **Assam.**

Sibsagar

Sibsagar was the capital of the Ahom kings. This is where Sukhapa found the water most suitable for wet rice cultivation. Relics of this great dynasty remain

Charaideo : Located around 28 kms east of Sibsagar, was the original capital of the Ahom Kings built by Sukhapa the founder of the dynasty. Charaideo is famous for its tombs of the kings and members of the royal family as a burial ground. Most of them were built of stones and bricks and are now in ruins.

Gaurisagar Group : 16 km south of Sibsagar on the Assam Trunk Road is the Gaurisagar tanks built by Queen Phuleswari in the year 1723. This spring fed tanks covers an area of 150 acres under water and on its banks stand three temples dedicated to Devi, Shiva and Vishnu.

Gargaon Palace : The principal town of the Ahom Kings, constructed by the 15th Ahom King Suklemnung in 1540. The palace lies 13 kms east of Sibsagar. The present seven storied edifice was built by King Rajeshwar Singha around 1762. All the underground stories and passages were blocked by the East India Company. The magazine made of bricks is within the palace compound and further eastward are two old stone bridges constructed by King Gadadhar Singha.

Sibsagar Tank and Temples : The tank was dug around 200 years ago. The tank is fed by natural springs and is surrounded by deep ditches and earthen moats. Three temples are built on its bank - Siva temple, Vishnu temple and Devidol temple.

Joysagar Tank and Temple : Historical records reveal that the tank was constructed in 45 days at Rangpur in 1697. The tank stands on the area of 318 acres half of which is under water and on its banks stand the Jeydol (Vishnu) temple, Shiva temple and Devi Ghar and Ghanashyam (Nati Gosain) temple.

Talatal Ghar : Built in 1699 by king Rudra Singha is located about 6 km away from Sibsagar. It is an underground garrison having three stories the lowest connected with Dikhow river by tunnel.

Rang Ghar : The Ahom Kings watched elephant fights and other sporting events from this two - storied, oval-shaped pavilion built by king Pramutta Singha.

assam.the Golden Valley

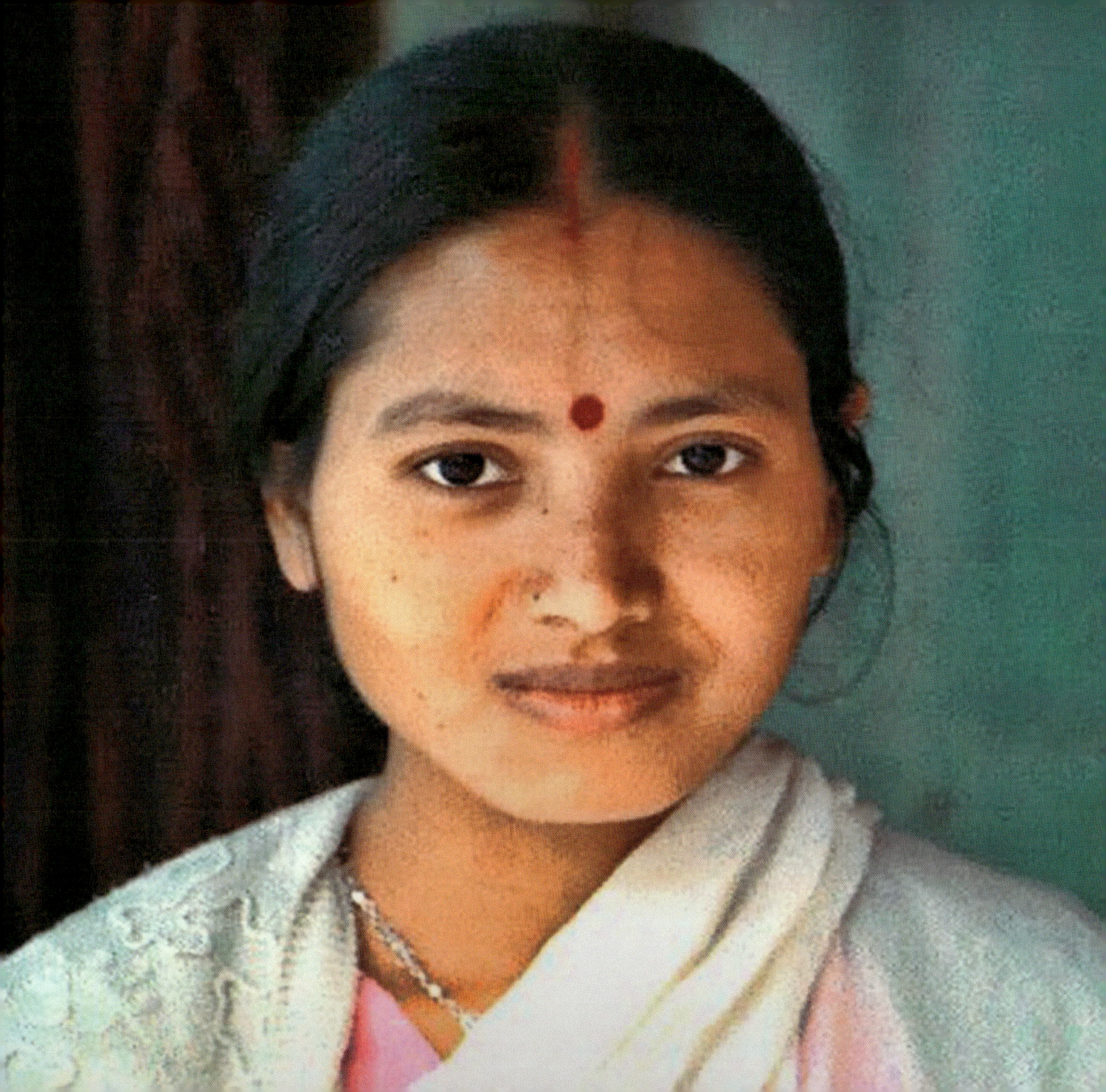

Sibsagar
The Ahom Kingdom
1228-1824

assam, the Golden Valley

talatal Ghar

Gola Ghar

Gorgaon Palace

Ranghar

assam,the Golden Valley

Jagganath Ghar

Joy Sagar

Sibsagar Circuit House

Shivadol

THE AHOM DYNASTY

courtesy Tai Ahom

1. Sukapha 1228–1268
2. Suteupha 1268–1281
3. Subinpha 1281–1293
4. Sukhangphaa 1293–1332
5. Sukhrangpha 1332–1364
6. Sutupha 1364–1376

Interrupted 1376–1380

7. Tyao Khamti 1380–1389

Interrupted 1389–1397

8. Sudangpha 1397–1407
9. Sujangpha 1407–1422
10. Suphakpha 1422–1439
11. Susenpha 1439–1488
12. Suhenpha 1488–1493
13. Supimpha 1493–1497
14. Suhungmung 1497–1539
15. Suklenmung 1539–1552
16. Sukhamphaa 1552–1603
17. Susenghpha 1603–1641
18. Surampha 1641–1644
19. Sutyinpha 1644–1648
20. Sutamla 1648–1663
21. Supungmung 1663–1669
22. Sunyatpha 1669–1673
23. Suklampha 1673–1675
24. Suhung 1675
25. Gobar 1675
26. Sujinpha 1675–1677
27. Sudaipha 1677–1679
28. Sulikpha 1679–1681
29. Supatpha 1681–1696
30. Sukhrungpha 1696–1714
31. Sutanphaa 1714–1744
32. Sunenpha 1744–1751
33. Surampha 1751–1769
34. Sunyeopha 1769–1780
35. Suhitpangpha 1780–1795
36. Suklingpha 1795–1810
37. Sudinpha 1810–1818
38. Purandar Singha 1818–1819

Burmese Rule 1819-1824

assam,the Golden Valley

Chairaideo
the ahom tombs

Shankardev.
1449-1568 C

The identity, Assamese, as a culture, was conceived, enumerated and established by *Shrimanta Shankardev*. King *Sukhapa* had unified the valley settlers, yet its cultural identity was fragmented, dominated by the prevailing beliefs practiced by the Mong Mao settlers.

Born in 1449, to the *Bar-Bhuyan* family at a Village named Alipukhuri near the town of Borduwa. The parents were *Kayasta* and possibly *Shakti* worshippers. Since he lost his parents early he was brought up by his grandmother *Khersuti*. He attended the local school, *Chhatrashal* of a renowned scholar *Mahendra Kandali* and wrote his first poem at the age of 11, which is sighted as an example of his sprouting genius. He grew up to be a strapping lad who, it is fabled, could swim across the mighty Brahmaputra, at spate.

He left school early and moved to Burduwa to take up his duties as a *Shrimoni* or the head of the *Bor-Bhuyan* family. Being artistically adept he wrote his first play, *Harishchandra upakhyan* here. This was followed by the production of a dance-drama, *Cihna yatra* The Script, the music and the scenes were written by his individually, the backdrops colouerd and even the design-assisted musical instruments were played by him.

In Borduwa he established a prayer house called *Harigriha* in which he installed a idol of *Lord Vishnu*, which was uncovered while digging the site for the temple. This *Harigriha* is still there. It was a treasure trove of his individual artistic flare adorned with books, musical instruments and his paintings.

In this period he married, *Suryawati,* who he lost very early, during the childbirth of his daughter, *Manu*. This left the impression of the fragility of life and he moved into religious introspection.

As soon as his daughter turned nine in the year 1482, he married her to *Hari* , handed over the management of his family affairs to his uncles and left for a pilgrimage to the *Vaishnava* religious centers of *Dwarka, Mathura, Brindavan, Gaya, Ayodhaya, Rameshwaram*. At *Badrikashram* he wrote his first *Bargeet(Religious Chant)* in *Brajavali*.

He returned after 12 year. During the period his family had moved back to Alipukhuri. On his grandmother's insistence he married again at the age of 44, a woman called Kalindi. After a short sojourn he moved back to *Borduwa* and established the first *Namghar*, prayer hall. During the period he received a copy

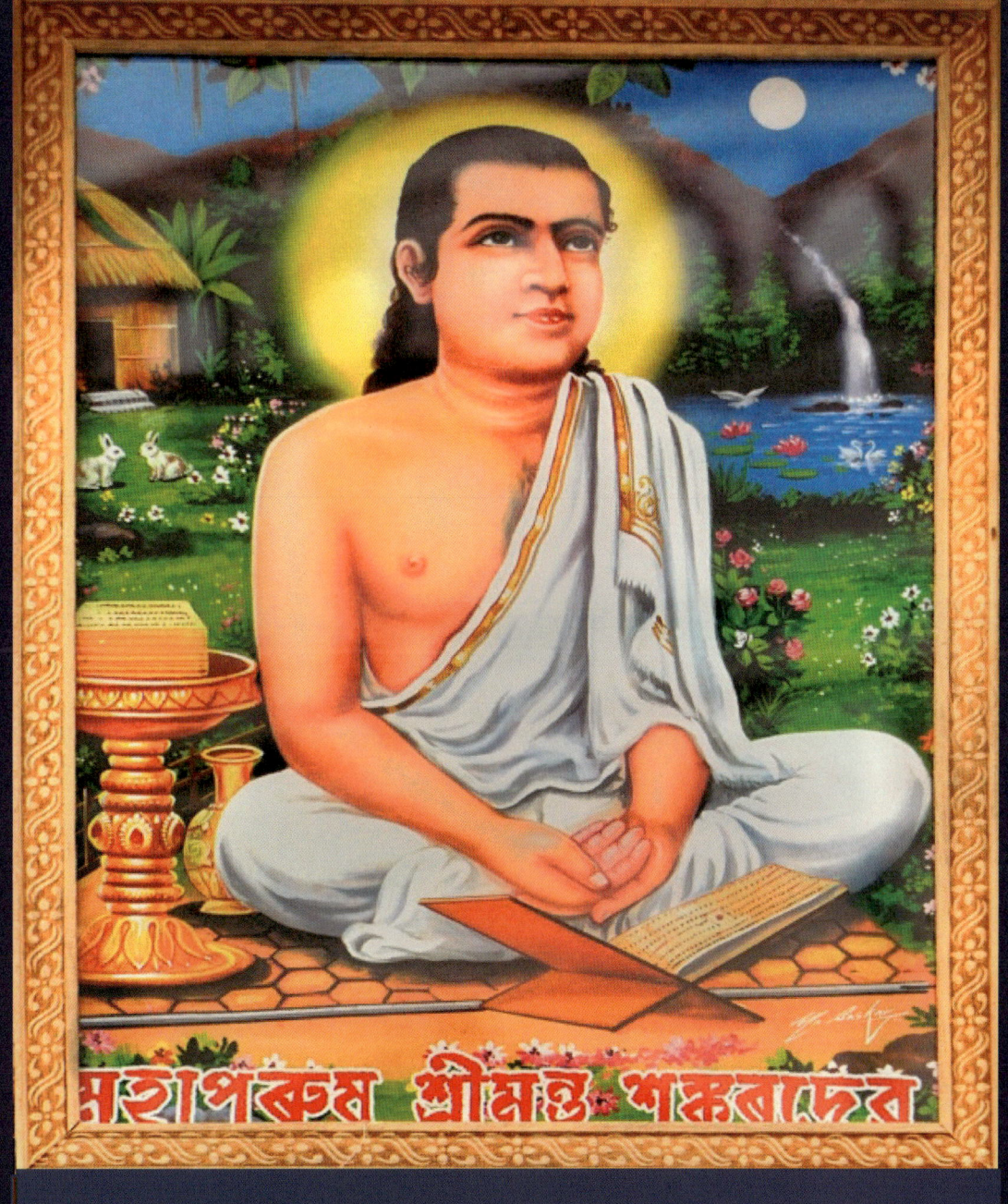

Artists impression of Sri Sri Sankardeo

of *Bhagwat Purana* from from Jagadisa Misra of Tirhut which had in it commentaries from Sridhara Swami of Puri, an *Advaita* scholar. He spent 13 years hereafter to customize the Gita to address the ethical and religious needs of the local people.

Shankerdev established this new *Mahapuruxiya dharma* which unlike the renaissance of *Vishnuism* sprouting all over India, propagated *Eka Sarana*, which was the worship of Lord Krishna individually and not in association with *Radha* His consort. There was a conflict on between the *Ahom* and the indigenous *Koch* kingdoms during the time and he moved to various locations, finally arriving at *Dhuwahat--Belguri*, which today exists and is renowned by the name of **MAJULI** island.

At *Majuli* he met his staunchest critic, *Madhadev* a staunch believer of *Shaktism*. They both being ardent worshippers and religious leaders of the time debated the two prevalent streams of religion of the times, till *Shankardev* could convince *Madhavdev* of the philosophy of *Eka Sarana*. There after Madhavdev became his staunchest supporter. The universality of the new religion was very appealing as it accepted into its fold people of all casts and beliefs and as such was immediately accepted by the people. Once the core was established, *Shankerdev* set up *Namghars* all over Assam. Shankardev wrote and enacted many dance-dramas eulogizing the benefits of the new religion, in fact it was the main media for propogating the rejuvenated belief, much to the chagrin of the prevalent Brahmins, who till then thought were the sole custodians of God.

These institutions, *Namghars*, eventually became the center of worship, communication and actually the community centers of the day. The preparation for these dance-drama routines brought the people together and uncovered the latent talents in acting, music, arts and crafts and overall a place for community development. Eventually it was institutionalized as a school for developing these arts along with traditional education and the concept of *Satra* evolved. Even today these *Satras* exist all over Assam are especially worth visiting in *Majuli*, where they are still preserved in its originality. To date, children are sent to live as celibates in these institutions and to learn the cultural graces of the Assamese society.

Due to the conflict with the Brahmins, *Shakardev* was politically targeted and he and his entourage had to move from *Majuli*. He continued to write and produce many plays and songs and dance dramas, but lost his son-in-law, who was imprisoned and executed and *Madhavdev* was imprisoned for over a year

Borduwa
The beginning

until the allegations were addressed and qualified to the ruling monarch of the time.

Shankardev and *Madhavdev* during these years moved to **PATBAUSI,** near the present day town of Barpeta and established their *Satras* there under *Thakur Ata's* hospitality. At the *kirtanghar* in Barpeta Some of the better known people he initiated into this new form of religion were *Chakrapani Dwija* and *Sarvabhauma Bhattacharya, Brahmins* by caste; *Ketai Khan,* a *kayastha; Govinda,* a *Garo; Jayarama,* a *Bhutia; Murari,* a *Koch* and *Chandsai* a *Muslim.* He befriended *Ananta kandali,* a well known scholar of Sanskrit, who translated parts of the *Bhagavata Purana* for him.

Damodardeva, another *brahmin*, initiated by *Sankaradeva* became the founder of the *Brahma Sanghati* sect of Sankaradeva's religion *Mahapuruxiya dharma.*
He stayed here for almost 18 years, during which he wrote various plays and *Borgeet* and continued translation of the epics. Again complaints were made against his conversion of people to the king at Kochbehar. In all he wrote 240 compositions of which only 34 exist as the others were destroyed in a fire.
He decide to go on another pilgrimage with an entourage of 170 people but returned within six months from Puri on his wife's request.
The situation had deteriorated as complaints were made to the King about his conversion of people to the new faith. *Shankardev* went into hiding. Many of his follower were subjected to extreme torture but they did not divulge his whereabouts. Eventually, through General *Chilarai,* a relative, an audience was arranged with the King. *Shankerdev* arrived at the audience reciting one of his extempore Sanskrit hymns followed by his own composition of one of the *Borgeet.*

The King was suitably impressed and after long discussions, all charges against him were dropped. In fact the king wanted to convert to this new religion. The king hereon wanted *Shankardev's* advise on many of the state matters and *Shankardev,* now an old man had to shuttle between Patbausi and Koch Behar.
Shankardev's renaissance vaishnuite religion of *Eka Sarana* became the moral fiber of the life and culture of the Assam valley established by the Ahom King Sukhapa. The dance-drama routine is still practiced and the *borgeets* resound the evening sunsets in every town till date. The Satriya dance form is recognized as an individual form at the National level and exponents travel far and wide across the globe demonstrating it.

32

Nestled in a corner of the North East on the river Brahmaputra is one of the largest fresh water island in the world called '**Majuli**' an admixture of culture, '**Satras**', dance dramas, celibate disciples, a laic lifestyle; upholding the essence of the Assamese culture. Although, time has moved on and most of the district towns in the North East have transformed into mini metropolises, not so the Island of *'Majuli'*

Arrive at Guwahati, from where you can either fly or drive down to Jorhat on the south bank of the river or Lakhimpur on the north bank. Board the ferry at Niamatighat in Jorhat for an hour and forty five minutes motorboat ride on the Brahmaputra to Kamalabari on the island. If lucky, you sight occasional fresh water dolphins and in winter swarm of migratory birds. No matter what hour of the day, the crossings are always exciting as you intermingle with the residents ferrying necessities to and fro from their island home. Season permitting you can also cross the river Subansiri from Lakhimpur to get to the island, a shorter crossing but a more tedious road journey.

Alighting from the boat you step into a picture-perfect world of neatly tended houses, seasonal birds, tropical flowers and a horizon of rice fields. It is an introduction to the rural simplicity. The mornings are early and crisp, progressing from the haze enshrouded dawn to the lighting of the cooking fires, the tinkling of cow bells, the barking of dogs or the exciting laughter of children. The day advances into sounds of utensils and clicking of home looms, the chirping of birds or the occasional snort of the buffalos tilling the land. The dusk is early and soothing. It is as though the island over the years has developed its own charismatic moods.

Majuli is home to some of the better known 'Satras' established by the propagators of the Assamese school 'Neo-Vaishnavism', **Shankerdev, Madhavdeva, Damodardev**, in the 15th and 16th century and governed today by *"goxain iswars"*, the head of the institution.

Majuli
Quintessentially Assamese

The satras are famed not for their grandeur but their simplicity.
During the renaissance of organized religion in India, Shankerdev (1449-1568) was born in Assam. He propagated this Philosophy so successfully through his dance-drama routine, that at one time the whole of the Brahmputra valley and its adjacent areas turned to Vaishnuism; be it the King or the other ethnic residents.

Shankerdev dissipated the caste system and unified all. His celibate disciples, especially groomed in the essence of the religion carried the message forward and it's practices by means of schools run by the priests themselves.

Besides religion, these schools also imparted education and training in the arts and the ethics of life. The teachers were the practicing priests hence, the facilities were built around the local temple for convenience.

Over the years the temple with its schools, auditoriums, its meeting and prayer rooms and the hostels became the center of religion, culture and education. In fact the life revolved around these campuses called 'Satra'. Such centers mushroomed all over and became the epicenters of life in Assam. The Patronage may have declined over the years but the practice continues till date.

At one time there were over a 100 'Satras' in Majuli of which only 22 exist today. The most prominent ones being, Dakhinpat, Aunieity, Kamalabari, Benganaati, Samuguri. These institutions are also custodians of the artifacts, jewellery, coinage, gifts from oversea, and other historical memorabilia. Each one holds on to a collection worth a museum. Some of the most interesting collection is the 'Bhagwat' hand written and dance movements hand painted on scrolls, parchment paper, even on ivory. A must see heritage.

Some of these 'Satras' have built guest-houses for convenience of researchers and historians either working or experiencing the lives of the in-house celibates. It is a novel experience.

With the advent of modernization, ferries are motor propelled, 'Saki' illumination is replaced by electricity and carts are being replaced by pollution emitting cars and busses. Although education is propagated by its almost 200 schools and over two dozen colleges,

One wonders if it is as complete as in the *Satras?*

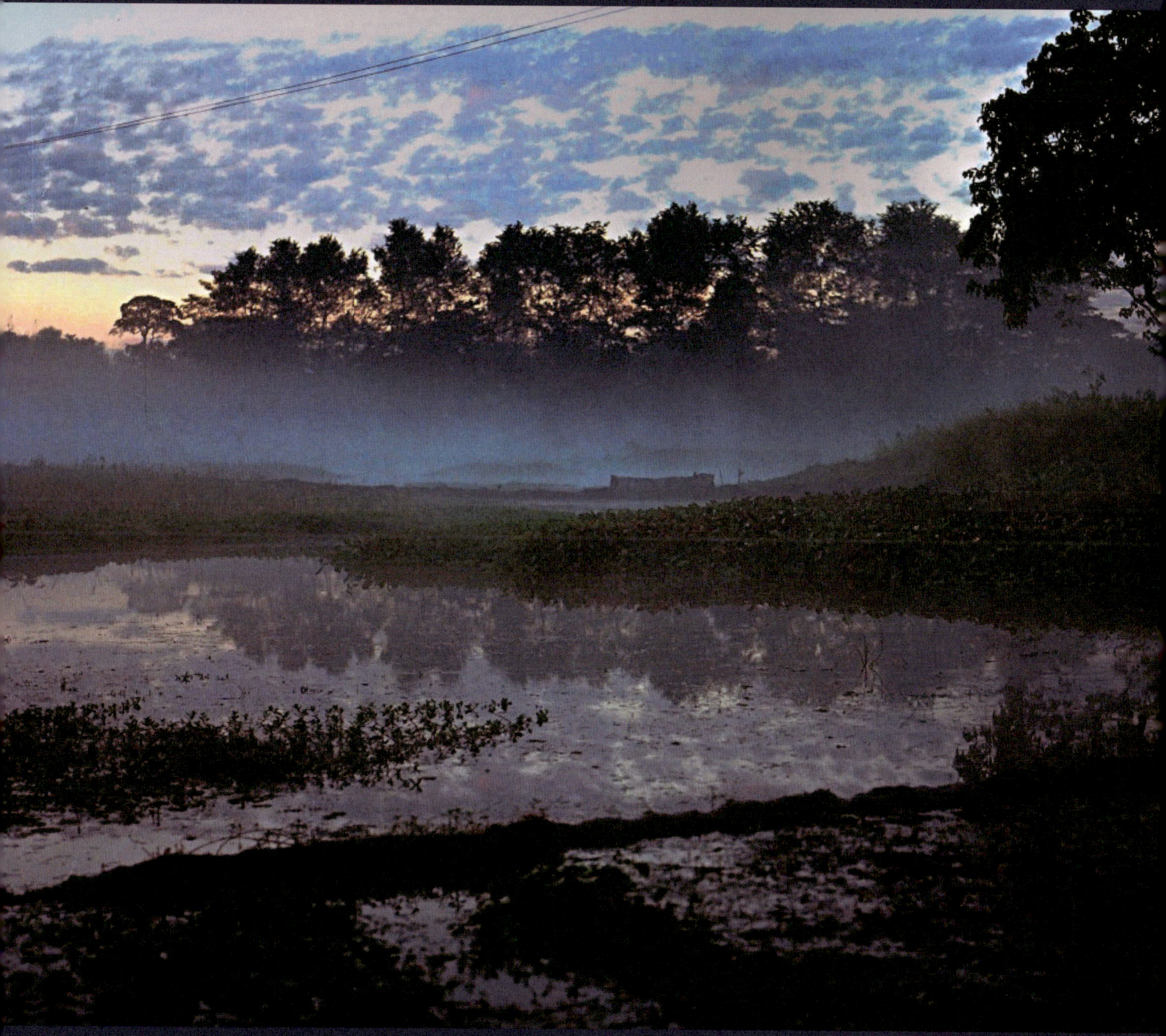

The materialistic 21s century life is pervading the old-world charm, but fortunately in greater measure the ethical culture; the essence of *Majuli,* prevails. Crops, in majority, grown on the loess brought by the floods with minimal addition of chemicals,houses are built with bio-recyclable materials and fresh water is available in plenty. The island is a tropical jungle and most of its trees serve a purpose, there is even a .*sar gos'* whose leaves and trunk serve as a natural fertilizer. All the animals, brought for a purpose, serve the populace well, assisting their daily chores or providing norishment. It is also home to numerous species of migratory birds in winter, sheltering in gay abandon, flocking the sky at dawn and dusk. Culture is the essence of all communities, so predominant in *Majuli*.

Regardless of its origin, all festivals are celebrated with such" joy that the whole island comes alive with smiling faces, colorful clothes, danceing, singing, feasting, and camaraderie all over.I t is one place where the various ethnic cultures - the Mishings, Deoris, Assamese, Kachari, Nepali, Kumar Haris, Kaibartas living in harmony, have evolved their own refinement; some call it the '*Majulian* culture'.

It is a remarkable experience to watch the sowing of crops, the fishing in ponds, the extensive use ,of Banana, bamboo, cane; in food and in furniture, the traditional designs' being woven at the home looms, the intricacies of producing the silk and cotton strands at home. Experience the old-world charm of attending to the household chores. Sharing the warmth of the cooking fires, grinding wheels of the husking mills.Taste the local cuisine, brew and desserts, observe the young *·Bhagats'* training in their dance, singing and *Naam-kirtan'* routine. Witness the production of the *·Bhagvat'* opera during the festival of '*Raas/* when the whole island turns into a stage and everyone in '*Majuli*' gets involved in the production of a most spectacular display of religious festivity seen anywhere in the World,

various Satras of Majuli

38

aspects of life in Majuli

40

assam,the Golden Valley

cultural wealth of Majuli

The heritage and culture of Barpeta District is predominated by the remarkable work of the great Assamese renaissance figure and reformer Mahapurush Shrimanta Sankardeva who laid the foundation of Assamese culture and heritage. Subsequently the great saints disciples namely Madhabdev, Haridev, Damodardev continued the tradition.

Sataras

Satras founded by these great saints and scholars that are considered regional-cultural institutions or monasteries that had a deep impact on the Social, political, economy of the region. Although the Satra institutions were established for the propagation of Vaishnuism, with passage of time these institutions transformed into open universities all-embracing socio-cultural centers for education, music, dance, sculpture, drama, fine-art and crafts.

Some of the important Satras are:

- Patbaushi
- Ganakkuchi
- Jania
- Sundaridia
- Barpeta
- Baradi
- Kanara

Patbaushi Satra

The Satra at Patbaushi was established by Shrimanta Sankardeva. Here the guru spent 18 years of his life with achievements including completion of the 'Kirtan Ghosa' and composition of twenty invaluable Borgeets. Some of the items used by these Gurus and Sachipat puthis are well-preserved here. The Satra is located about two km north of Barpeta town.

Barpeta
The cultural centre of Lower Assam

Sankerdev Satra

44

Ganakkuchi Satra

This satra was founded by Sri Madhab Deva for which the land was purchased by Shrimanta Sankardeva for 1 Gold and nominated his close disciple Shri Madhab Deva as the satradhikar to stay here to spread his faith and he went on to stay here for eighteen long years. Some of the items used by the guru and Sachipat puthis are well-preserved here. The Satra is located within Barpeta town area.

Jania Satra

This Satra was established by Sankardeva's disciple Shri Narayan Das Thakur Ata. He composed a large number of devotional songs here. This Satras located at a distance of 8 km from Barpeta in Barpeta Jania Road,

Sundaridiya Satra

The Satra was established by Shri Madhab Deva after leaving Ganakkuchi Satra. The first satradhikar of Barpeta Satra Sri Mathura Das Burha Ata initially came to this Satra and became a disciple of Shri Madhab Deva. It was here that Paal Nam and Beer Nam or Thiya Nam was created by Sri Madhab Deva. A large number of items used by the guru including Sachipat-puthis are preserved here.

Barpeta Satra

Sri Madhab Deva founded the Barpeta Satra and stayed here for 8 long years. Here he appointed Sri Mathura Das Burha Ata as the first Satradhikar of the Satra. It was Burha Ata who systematised the administration of the Satra leading to development of the institution and the region of Barpeta. A democratic system was introduced which is effective till today.

Large number of followers came to Barpeta to convert to the Vaishnava faith irrespective of their caste that created an egalitarian Society. In the 'Bhajghar' a lamp is continuously burning for more than 400 years that is called 'Akhay Banti'. Sri Krishna Doul festival is organised at the premises of Doul ghar. Within the premises a cultural school, Keli kadam tree, Shri Shri Mathura Das Burha Ata Library, study-room, office and kitchen are also located. Constitution formulated by Sri Mathura Das Ata is still in vogue.

Baradi Satra

This satra was also established by Sri Madhab Deva and stayed here for a very short period. The Sankarite culture spread far and wide from Baradi making it a centre for learning. The place is located about 2 km east of Barpeta town.

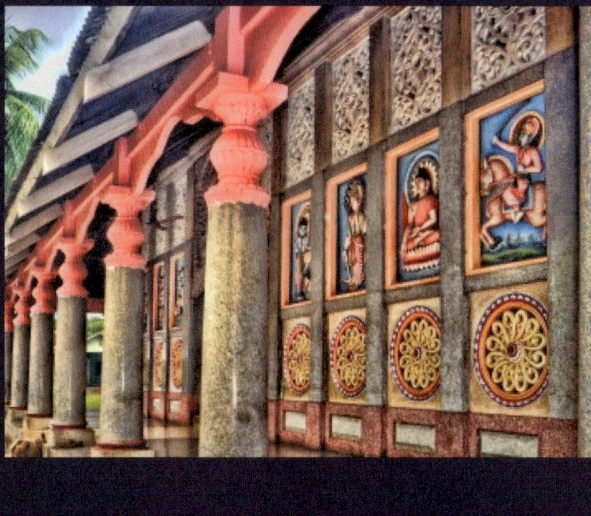

Barpeta Satra

The great cultural Saint Srimanta Sankardeva created different art forms that became integral part of Assamese culture.

Borgeet

Devotional songs composed by Shrimanta Sankardeva are still popular in this region.

Ankiya Geet

Shrimanta Sankardeva composed ankiya geet for ankiya plays. These are sung on special occasions like Doul festival,and anniversaries of the two gurus and other festivals.

Holi Geet

Holigeet are the unique form of chorus songs that originated in Barpeta satra and spread throughout the state. These are sung during the Doul festival.

Loka Geet

Kamrupi Loka geet is popular form of folk music that expresses thoughts and emotion of the common people. Beside this various forms of songs linking the day to day activities are also popular like songs for *biya*(marriage) geet, *now khelor*(boat race) geet, *maha-kheda* (mosquito driveout)geet, *lora-dhemalir*(child's play)geet, *boroshibowa* (fishing) geet, *nisukoni (lallabye)geet* and various forms of *bihu geet*.

Dances

Devadasi nritya was performed at Pari Hareswar Devalaya in Bajali, Deodhani nritya is another form. Shrimanta Sankdardeva popularised the *Satriya nritya* among the common people. Other dance form that the guru popularised are *Krishna nritya, Kalidaman nritya, Dasavatara nritya, Jhumura nritya, Sali nritya, Sutradhari nritya, Gopi nritya Raja Nritya, Rani nritya* . which were performed in the Satras. *Ojapali* is a popular dance form among the people.

Drama and Theater

Sankardeva popularised 'Bhaona' or mythological plays that became the centre of attraction for the common masses. Colorful dresses were worn by the participants on the occasion. These dramas resulted in formation of professional theatre groups. Large numbers of these theatre groups enjoy popularity among the people of Assam. Theatre groups have not only carved out a niche but also revolutionized this medium despite the challenge from Cinema Halls.

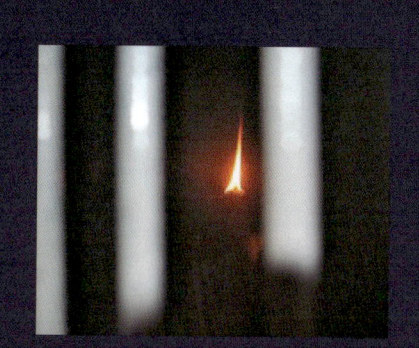

the lamp originally lit over 500 years ago

Handicraft

Decorative items of daily use including furniture, gift items, decoration pieces are prepared by rural artisans out of cane and bamboo.

Bell and Brass Metal Industry

The renowned town of Sarthebari is well-known for the household bell and brass-metal industry. Traditional utensils and fancy items designed by the artisans are found in every Assamese household. Most popular utensils here prepared are xorai for offering as gift to namghars and bota on which paan and betel nuts served to guests.

Pottery

Pottery works are popular among the common people. The Hira community is engaged in this profession. Ethnic and traditional items of daily use are prepared by the artisans.

Wooden Craft

Among the various articles preserved in the Satras, the decorative items made out of wood reflects the skilful artistry of the carpenters. On the Guru Asana or the pedestal various animals and birds are aesthetically carved by the artisans.

Mask

Bhaonas or plays introduced by Shrimanta Sankardeva used masks which are made of tribal art and folk element. These are prepared with materials like terracotta, pith, paper mache, metal, bamboo and wood.

Jewellery

Barpeta is famous centre for preparation of Traditional Assamese ornaments with Gold. The ornaments are still as popular the female community.

Paintings

Paintings are traced back to the medieval period. Paintings available in the Satras reflect the skilful work of the painters.

Ivory Carvings

Products including Ornaments, Toys, images of Gods and Goddesses, Animals, Comb are made by skilful artisans of Barpeta since the time of Shrimanta Sankardeva.

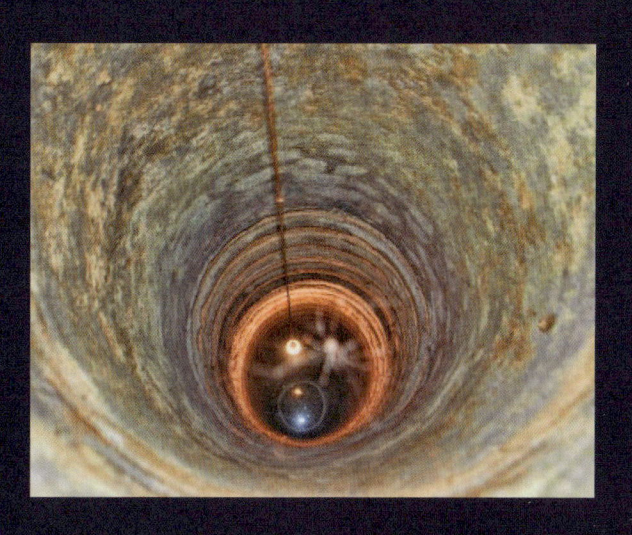

Sri Shankerdev's well

50

Satra reference terms:

Aldhara: Personal attendant of *Satradhikar* or superior monk.

Athpariya: Officer who keeps vigil at Satra (literally, having the eight stages of a day or night).

Bahar: Temporary camp for Satradhikar during his periodic visit to villages.

Bargeet: Devotional songs in classical tunes particularly composed by Sankaradeva and Madhavadeva.

Bayan: Officer-in-charge of instrumental music.

Bhagavati: Ecclesiastical officer engaged in reading and expounding the Bhagavata.

Bhajana: Higher form of ordination.

Bhakat: Monk; initiated disciple, celibate.

Bharali: Provision-keeper of a Satra.

Bhawana: Religious theatrical performance

Cari(pronounced Sari)-vastu: Four fundamental principles of Vaishunuite religion;
    deva (refuge in Lord Krishna),
    nama (glorification of God),
    guru (acceptance of a preceptor), and
    bhakat (good company for satsanga).

Carit-puthi: Biography of Vaishnava saint.

Damodariya: Followers of Damodaradeva who established the Brahmana-samhati.

Deka Adhikar: Vice-pontiff of Satra.

Deuri: Distributor of sacred offerings in religious gathering.

Gayan: Officer-in-charge of music and singing.

Guru: Preceptor.

Guru-kar: Tithe: religious tax or contribution.

Hatis: Group of huts.

Karapat: Gateways.

Kevaliya: Celibate monk.

Kirtan-ghar: Prayer-hall, term used mostly in Lower Assam.

Krishna-nac: Form of dance by Krishna.

Mahanta: Leader of Satra.

Mahapurushiya: Sankaradeva's sect.

Mahaprasad: Sacred offerings consisting of pulse, uncooked rice and fruit.

Manikut: Shrine: small alcove attached to Namghar where sacred books are placed on thapana, or singhasana.

Medhi, Raj-Medhi: Officers who periodically supervise the religious life of the disciples.
Mekhela: Woman's skirt.
Namghar: Prayer-hall; used mostly in Upper Assam. '
Nam-kirtan: Community singing in praise of god.
Pacani: Officer who collects tithes and contributions from disciples.
Padasila: Foot-prints (of Sankaradeva and Madhavadeva).
Pathak: Reciter of religious texts.
Prasanga: Religious service; matins.
Prasad: Sacred offering.
Saj-tola: Officer who collects contributions from disciples.
Samhati: Sect.
The four principal Samhatis are:
        Brahma-Samhati,
        Kala-Samhati,
        Nika-Samhati   and
        Purusa-Samhati.
Saran: Initiation.
Satra: Monastery.
Satradhikar: Head of Satra; pontiff.
Sisya: Laity/disciple
Singhasana: Wooden throne standing on four carved lions; sacred text is placed on it for worship.
Sravani: Devotees especially appointed to listen to reading and expounding of sacred texts at services.
Than: A place of worship
Thapana: Altar; place set up for worship.
Udasin: Unmarried; celibate.

assam,the Golden

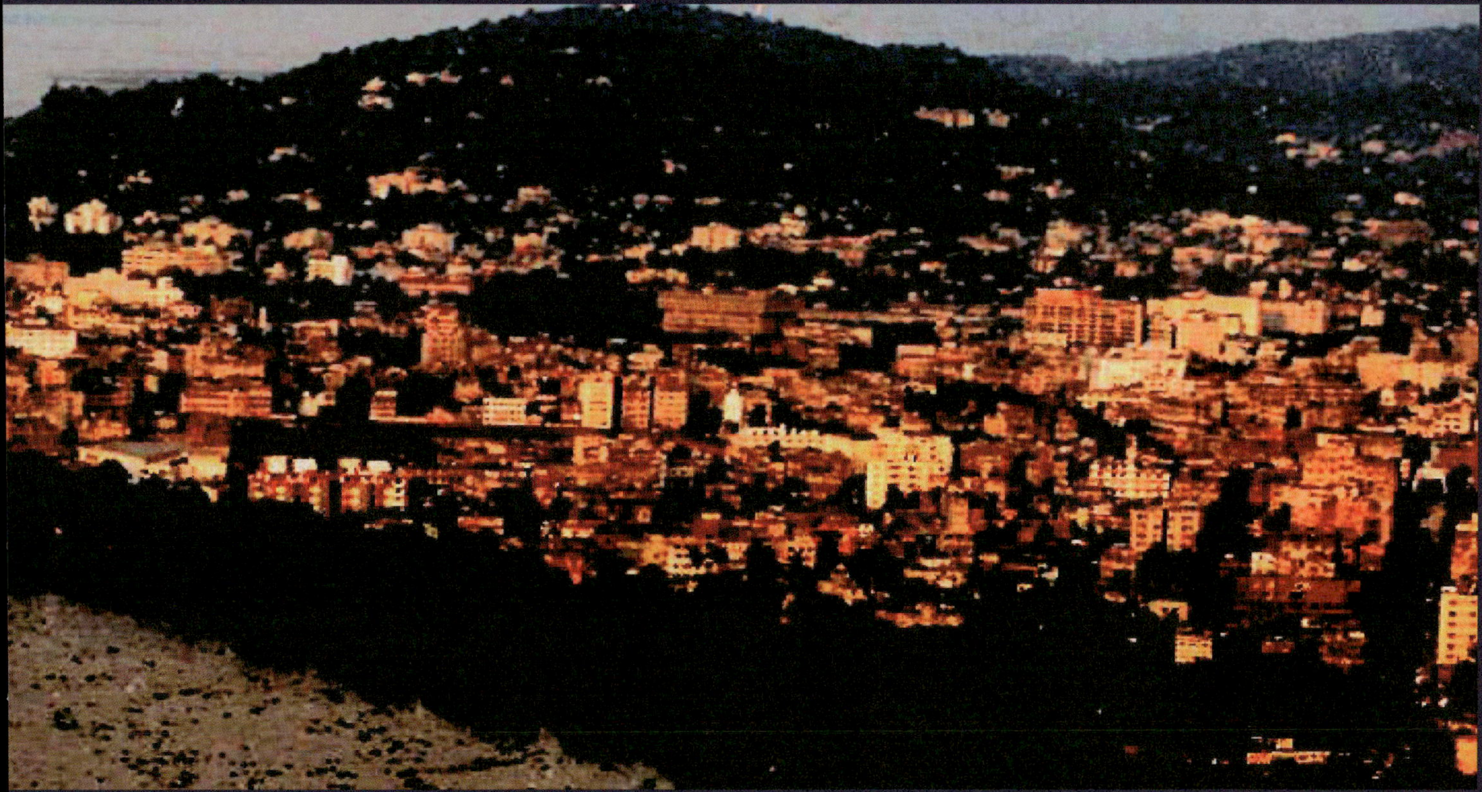

Guwahati

Till a few years ago one ferried across the Brhamaputra into Guwahati and the North East adventure began. The city historically known as Pragjyotispur the capital of Kamrupa, Is today ,the gateway to the region, well connected by road , rail and air to the rest of the country. It is forecasted to become the nodal point for international travel to the Far East. Indian Airlined flies regularly to Bangkok.

All incursions into the other states of the North are best started at Guwahati, since the North East is best seen by road and for the Jet-Set traveller, regular services of Indian Airlines/Arunachal helicopter service connect the city to some of the remotest towns.

The visitor is awed by the first sight of the mighty Brahmaputra and the inviolability of Trantrism, depicted at the Temple of Kamakhya on the top of the Nilachal Hills on the banks of the river. It is known as the Yoni Peeth. The resting place of the genitals of Sati the consort of Lord Shiva. A must for Hindu pilgrimage. Ambubacchi mela is held here very year in the month of Asar (Jun-July) when pilgrims from all over flock here.

Shankerdev Kalashetrs is a remarkable Cultural Centre, which gives you an insight into the cultural landscape of Assam, in fact in small measures of the whole North East, as most of the inhabitants of now politically demarked states have amalgamated into the Assamese societies over the centuries. The other places to visit is Baisitha , Ugratara, and Nabagraha, which is a temple dedicated to the planets.
Guwahati is well serviced by travel agents who along with their counterparts can fix you your Adventure ,Cultural or Leisure persuits in any of the other sister states. In fact today you can also take cruise down the Brahmaputra, to Kaziranga, the world famous game park on the 'Charaidew', a motor vessel , and see village life and other game sanctuaries on route .
The East has opened up a whole new world of hills in millions of colour of green and valleys of golden harvest , unseen in any other part of the world.

Kamakhya temple

Walkabout

Guwahati is the gateway, even today. As being the metropolis of the North East your onward journey starts here,by Train,Plane,Bus Taxi or self driven cars. In Assam, I am of the opinion, that your excursions would begin and end here. The state of Assam is bifurcated by the river Brahmaputra and as there are only three bridges most of the crossings, till recent times, was done on either steamers or boats. In some places the practice is prevalent more by need than by choice. So the cities/ towns are either on the North Bank or the South Bank.

From Guwahati you can make excursions to west or locally referred to Lower Assam or the East referred to as Upper Assam; the colonial terms continue. Game-parks and Tea gardens are spread all over the state and it also has the first Oil Derrick of India in Dgboi, the premier Oil town.

Going South one could plan to go to the historical centers of Barpeta,Manas Tiger Reserve, Goalpara, Surya Pahar,and Dhubri or via Meghalaya to Diphu. Halflong the only Hill station of Assam, and on to Silchar which borders Bangladesh.

Day excursions are possible to Hajo a cultural town,Sualkuchi the town renowned for its Silk and to Orang and Pobitara, the sanctuaries. Futher on the same circuit is Tezpur and Bhalukpung, famous for **Mahseer** fishing and Orchids of Arunachal Pradesh.

Upper Assam journeys would bring you to Kaziranga National Park, Sibsagar, Jorhat,Dibrugarh and on to Oil towns of Duliajan and Digbaoi. Should venture further on the beautiful Tea Garden fringed roads you would come to the Lido Road, and in a few years possibly, travel through to Myanmar, erstwhile Burma.

One thing is for sure as you discover Assam you will see Million shade of green vegetation, Golden colors of harvest, the serenity of Tea bushes and ever present songs of the birds.

It is God's own country blessed with some of the politest people in the world.

Nabagraha Temple

Basista Temple

Tara Temple

Kalashetra

Saraighat Bridge

assam, the Golden Valley

60

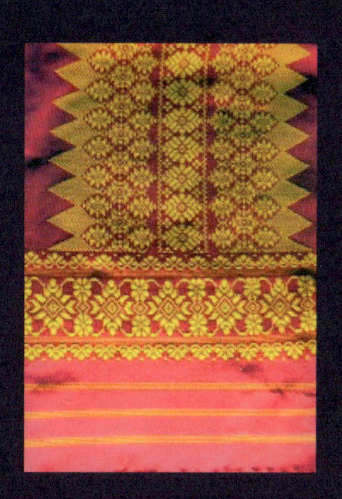

Madan Kamdev
Temple ruins

Madan Kamdev belonged to the 10th to 12th century A.D. when the Pala Dynasty ruled Kamrupa. The ruins are believed to be the remains of more than 20 temples consigned to Lord Shiva. The surviving portion of Madan Kamdev shows Kalpa-vriksha (the tree of fulfillment), six sided Bhairava, four headed Shiva, Demons, Serpants and men, women and animals in every conceivable erotic postures.These

assam,the Golden Valley

62

assam,the Golden Valley

Madan Kamdev

Orang
National Park

The Orang National Park is located on the north bank of the Brahmaputra River in the Darrang and Sonitpur districts of Assam. It covers an area of 78.81 square kilometers. It is similar to as both the parks have a similar landscape made up of marshes, streams and grasslands . The park is rich in flora and fauna, including One-Horned Rhinoceros, pigmy hog, elephants, wild Water buffalo and tigers. It is the

Pobitora Wildlife Sanctuary is situated at a distance of around 50kms from Guwahati and covers the area of both Kamrup and Nagaon district. The place was declared a sanctuary in the year 1971 so as to protect the famous Great Indian one horned Rhinoceros. The sanctuary covers an area of around 38.8square.kilometers. The best time for visiting the place is between the months of November-March.

Pobitara
National Park

Hajo
Amalgamation of Faiths

The **Hayagriva** temple at **Hajo** in Assam, 28 kilometers Guwahati enshrines Vishnu as Hayagriva (an incarnation of Vishnu in the form of a human being with a horse's head). The hillock on which this temple is housed is known as Manikoot Parvat.

Manikoota or Hajo has been a center of worship for both Hindus and Buddhists. While **Buddhists** regard the image of worship as that of **Buddha**, the Hindus regard it as that of **Vishnu** as Narasimha. The present structure of the temple dates back to the period of King **Raghudeva Narayana** of the 16th century CE. The stone temple built on a hillock consists the sanctum, the ardhamandapa and a mahamandapa said to have been constructed later by the ruler Nara Narayana. Carved on the exterior walls of the temple are life sized sculptures of the 10 **avataras** of Vishnu. In this representation, Buddha is also considered to be an incarnation of Vishnu

This ancient place is not only a holy place of the Hindus but also for the Muslims and the Buddhists as well. Thousands of devotees of each religion visit the place in every season of the year to pay homage to their pilgrims.

At a distance of about 5 KM from the great Hayagriba Madhaba Temple the well known Poamecca the old pilgrimage of the Muslims is situated. It is believed that Pir Ghiasuddin Aulia who built it brought soil from Mecca to place in the foundation of the shrine. Thus Hajo has become a place of religious tolerance since time immemorial and it can be said that the place has been standing as a symbol of ideal secularism since remote past in Assam.

The Hindus and the Buddhists assemble together in the Hayagriba Madhaba Temple to offer prayers. In Poamecca, the pilgrimage of the Muslims, the Hindus and Muslims together assemble on the day of Baisakha (middle of April to middle of May) and both the communities offer their prayers in the same place as per their own usages. The Buddhist pilgrims of Tibet and Bhutan consider the soil of Hajo as sacred soil like the water of the river Ganges for the Hindus and when they come for paying their holy homage to Hajo they carry a little soil of Hajo with them on their departure.

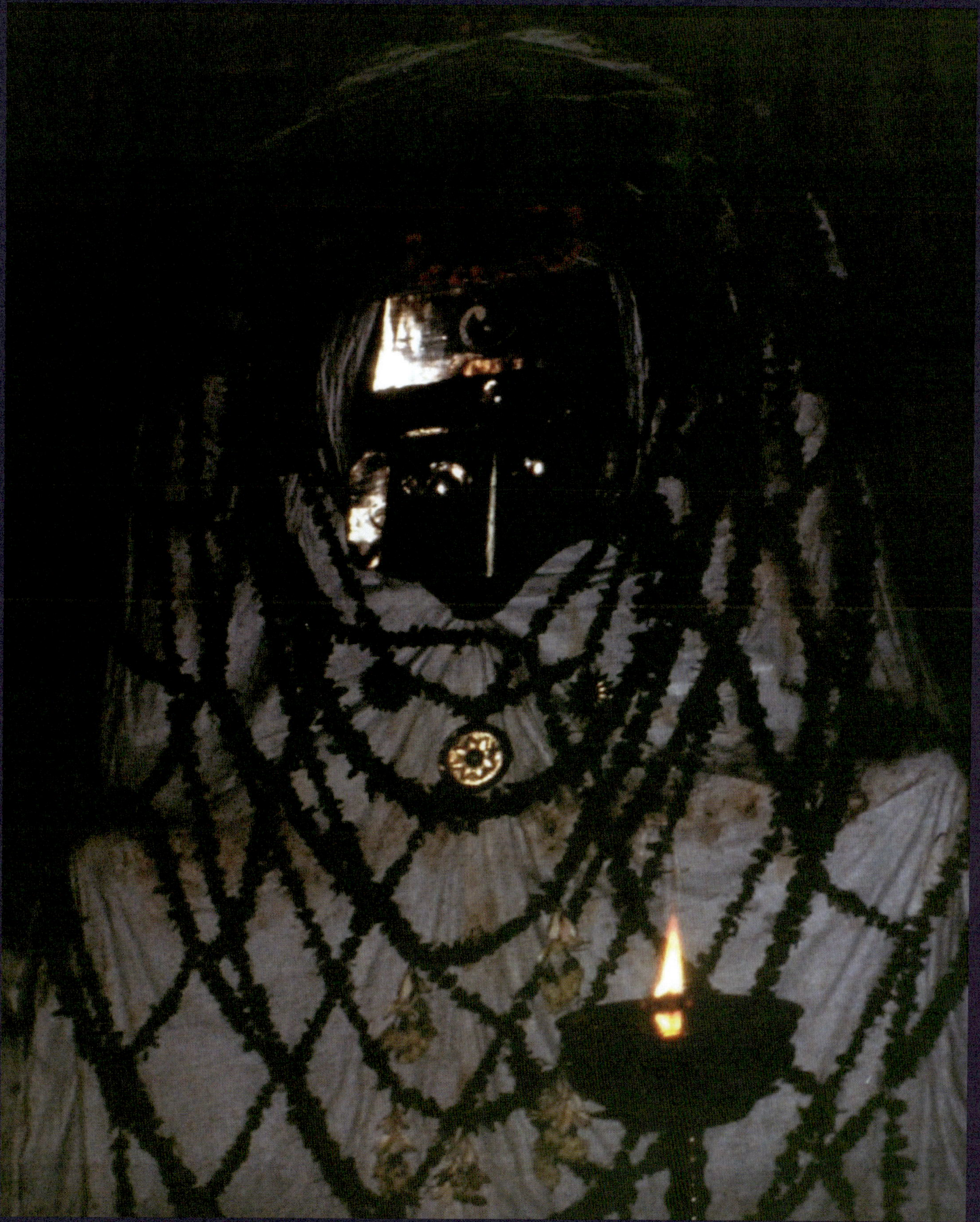

Hajo Hayagriva temple

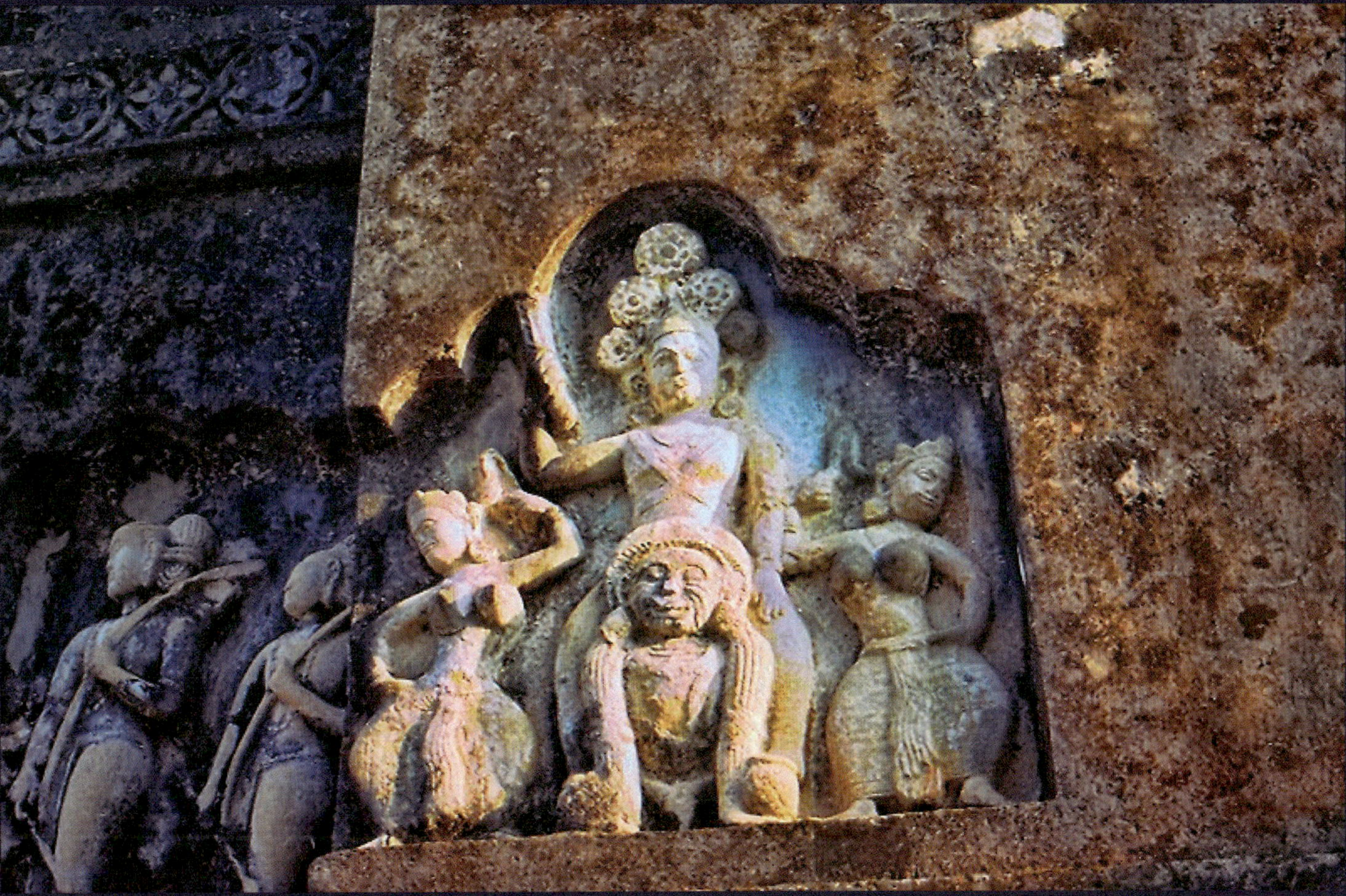

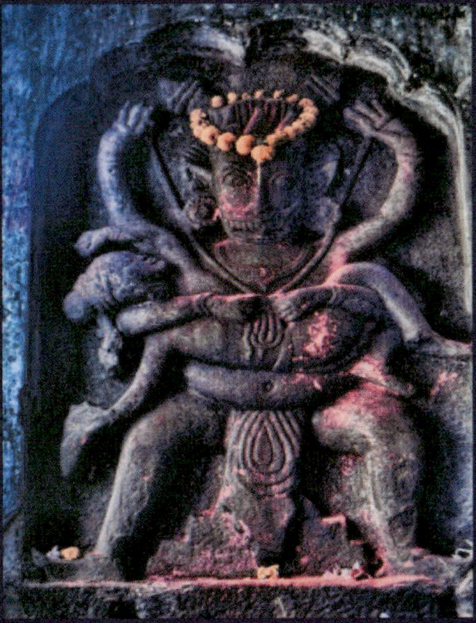

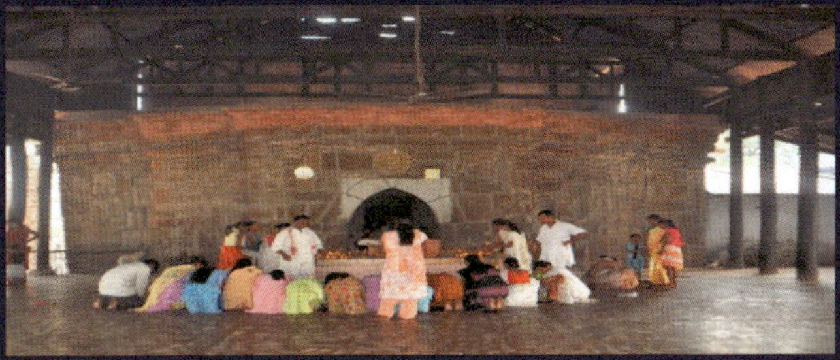

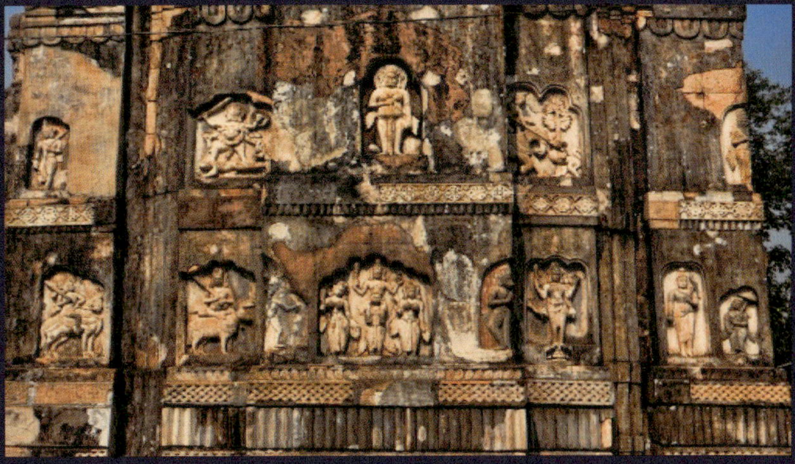

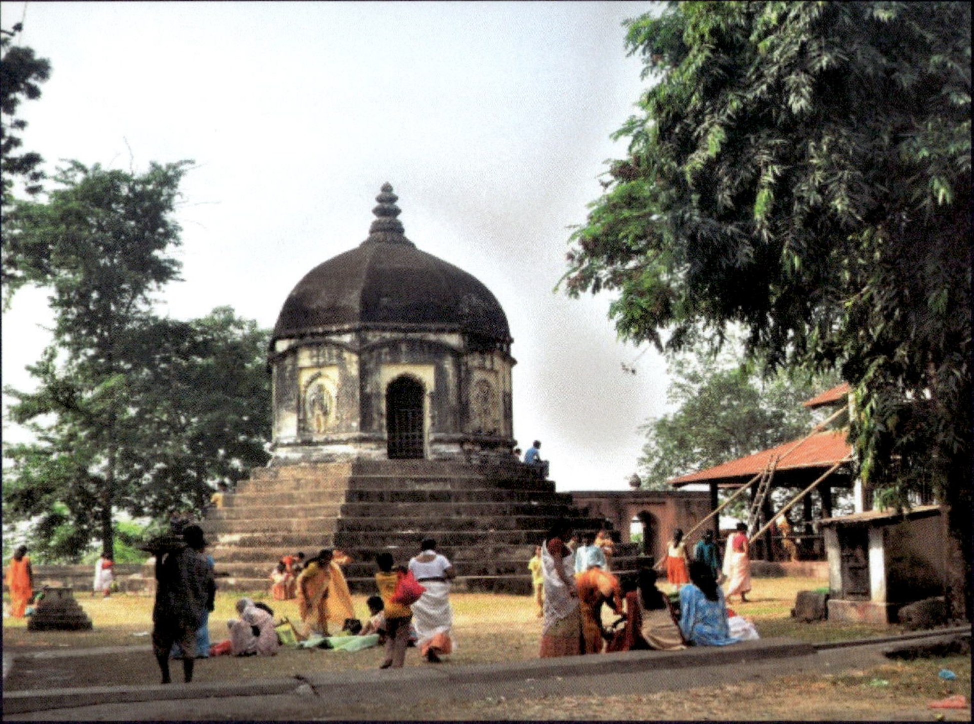

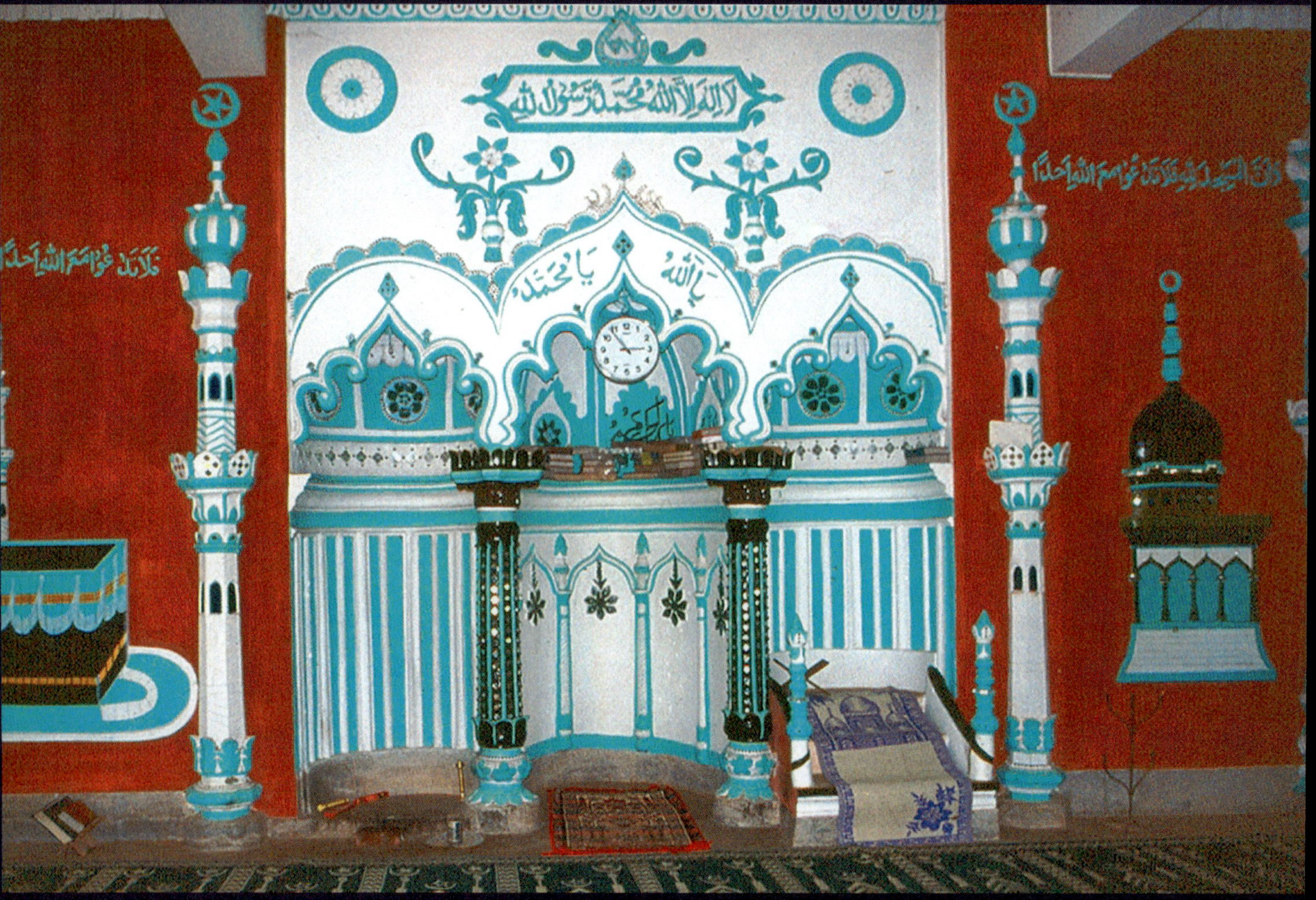
لا اله الا الله محمد رسول الله
يا محمد
يا الله

Pua Mecca

In 1322, a Muslim saint named Giasuddin Aulia had come to Kamrupa with the invading army of Sultan Giasuddin Bahadur Shah. It was Giasuddin Aulia Tabrizi who established the dargah at Pua Mecca in Hajo. It is believed that he had carried a handful of the holy soil from Mecca to consecrate this Durga.

Manas Tiger Reserve

Manas Tiger Reserve was created in 1973 at the time of the launch of the Project Tiger in India. The Reserve runs along the Indo-Bhutan international border, at par with the wildlife habitats in Bhutan. The river Manas flows from the gorges of Bhutan and splits into two major streams as it enters India. You are sure to see Tigers here and of course the beautiful Golden Langoor, which lives only around this sanctuary. Time permitting one can cross over to the Bhutan part of the sanctuary which houses the King's holiday resort.

In Manas one comes across sal forests, moist-deciduous forests, isolated patches of ever-green forests, riverine forests, grasslands of both savannah and terai types. Manas habitat provides an excellent abode to the tiger as well as it prey species: Hog deer, Sambar, Swamp deer, Asiatic wild buffalo and Gaur. These species migrate freely across the international border. The vegetation at the forest is a habitat for Capped Langur, golden Langur, Assamese Macaque, Rhesus Macaque, Common Langur, Slow Loris, Royal Bengal Tiger, Black Panther, Leopard Cat, Clouded Leopard, Wild Cat, Golden Cat, Fishing Cat, Large Indian Civet, Small Indian Civet, Common Palm Civet, Himalayan Palm Civet, Binturong, Common Mongoose, Small Indian Mongoose, Dhole, Jackal, Indian Fox, Red Fox, Himalayan Black Bear, Sloth Bear, Smooth Indian Otter, Yellow Throated Materna, Chinese Badger, Yellow bellied Weasel, Common Otter, Indian Pangolin, Bearded Sheathtailed Bat, Fulvous Fruit Bat, Short nosed Fruit Bat, Greater Yellow Bat, Three Stripped Palm Squirrel, Five Stripped Palm Squirrel, Malayan giant squirrel, Bay Bamboo Rat, Little Indian Field Mouse, Indian Porcupine, Asiatic Elephant, The Great Indian One Horned Rhinoceros, The Gaur, the Asiatic Water Buffalo, Sambar, Hog Deer, Barking Deer, Swamp Deer, Spotted Deer, Wild Boar, the Gangetic Dolphin

Circuit House within the park

Manas River

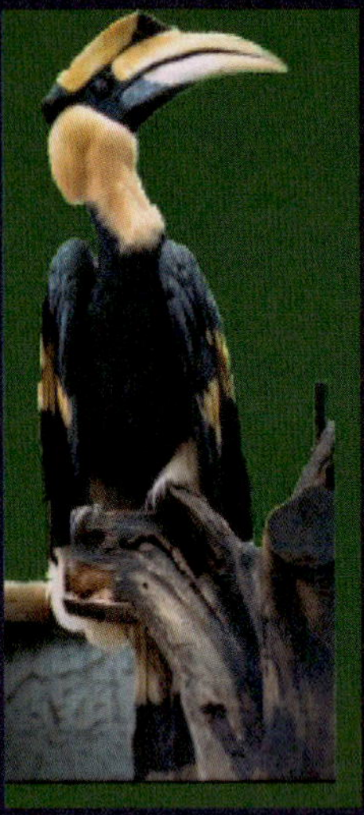

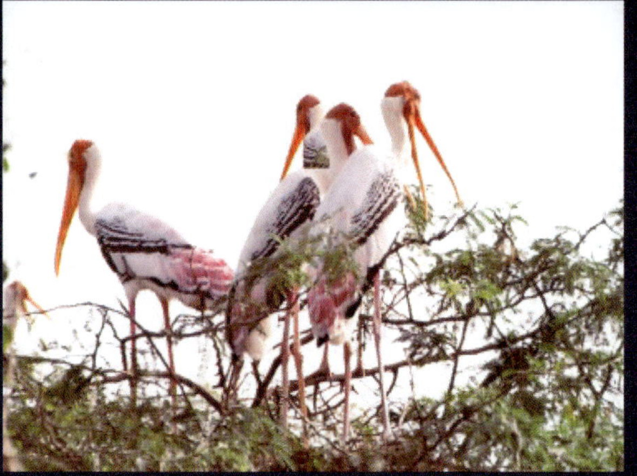

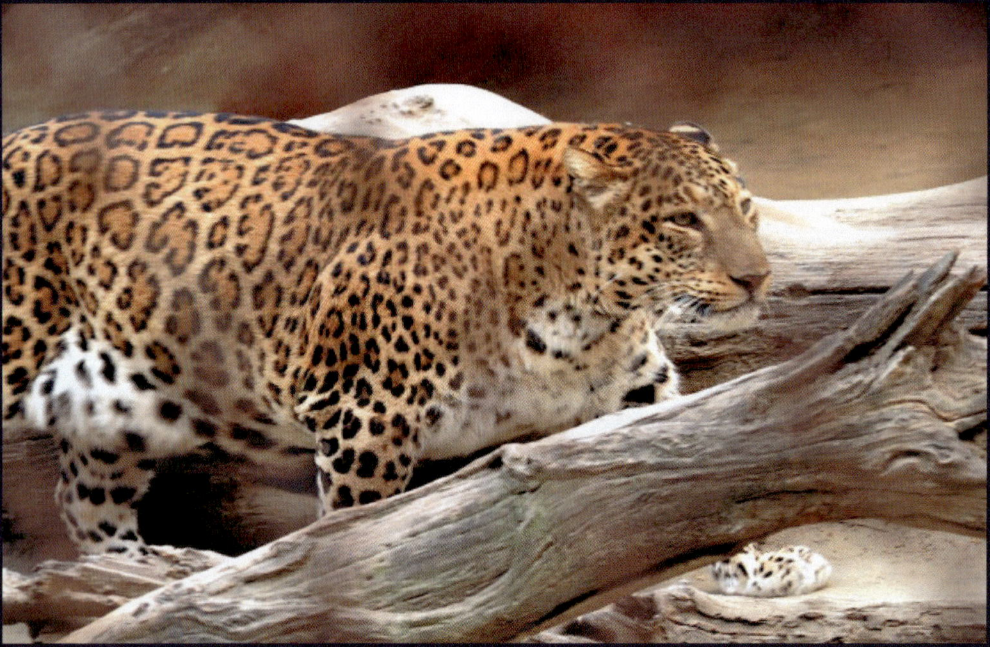

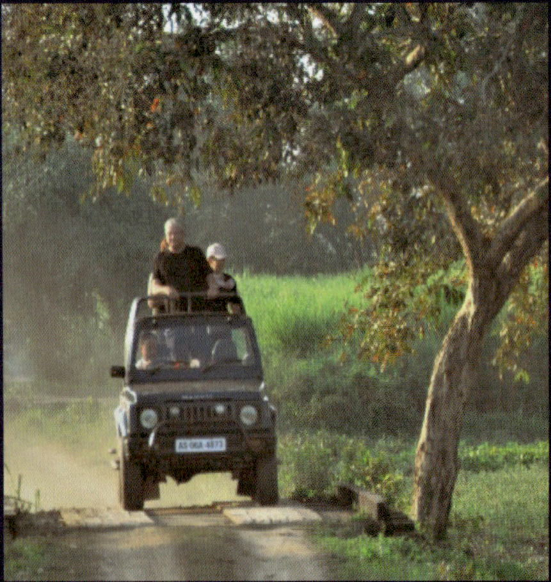

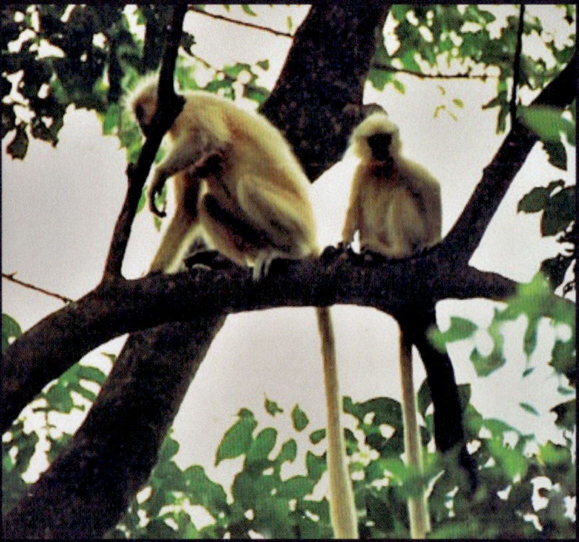

76

assam,the Golden Valley.

Surya Pahar

Surya Pahar

Surya Pahar,the abode of the sun as the name signifies is situated in the Goalpara District, normally 3/4 hours drive from Guwahati.

It is an interesting archeological site, in the sense it has remains of Hindu, Jain and Buddhist faith as seen from the carved engravings. It is believed that 100,000 ShivaLingas are stcattered all over the large site. Kalika Purana mentions that there were two such sites prevalent in Assam ,one of which is Surya Pahar.

Inside the temple, a carved stone slab is still worshipped as Surya. The inner circular carving has been identified as Prajapati. The outer circle includes twelve lotus petals, each seated with a figure of Aditya. The Adityas depict the twelve-solar divinity of Dharti, Mitra, Aryaman, Rudra, Varuna, Surya, Bhaga, Vivashan, Pushan, Savitri, Tvastri and Vishnu.Other fifures include the 12 armed Vishnu.

Among the identified Jain figures is one of the first Tirthankaras, Adinath, carved in sitting posture with two bulls in the base. In addition, the 25 votive stupas of different sizes show that there was Buddhist influence in Kamarupa and that too, earlier than many other parts of India.
It is an interesting site to visit as there are not many places in Assam which depict,Mahavira.

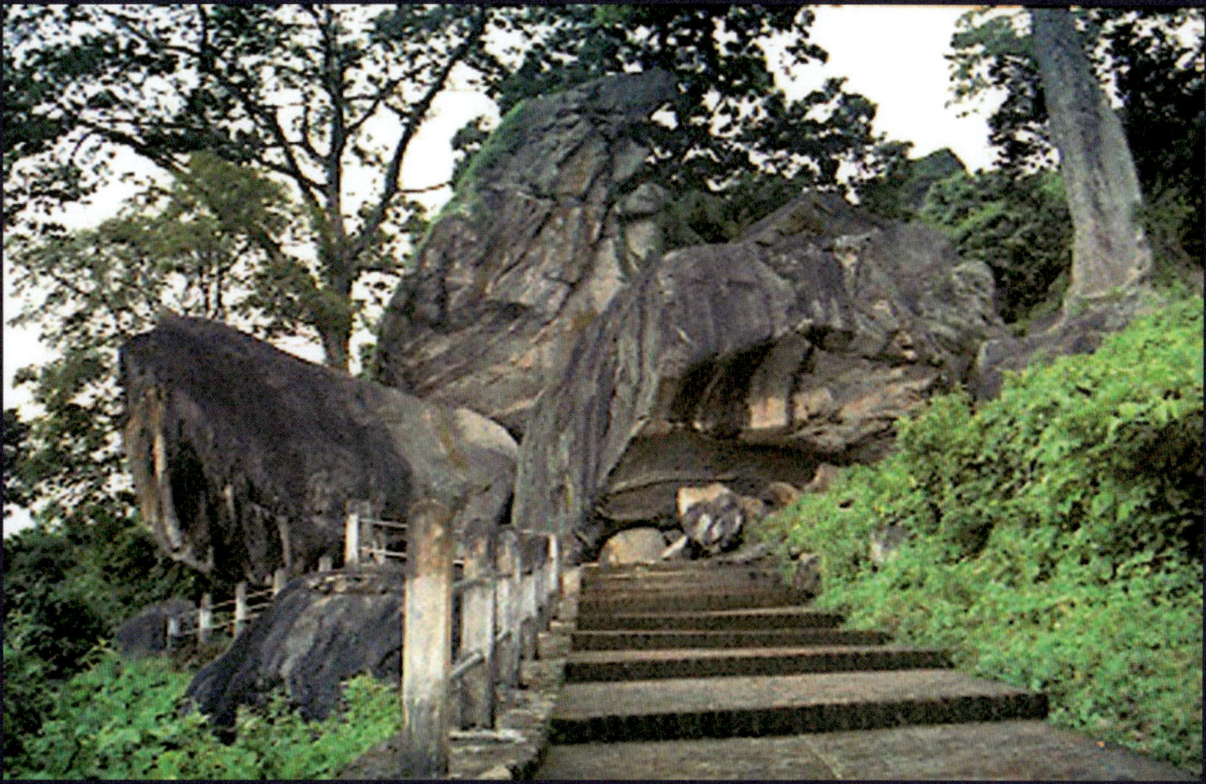

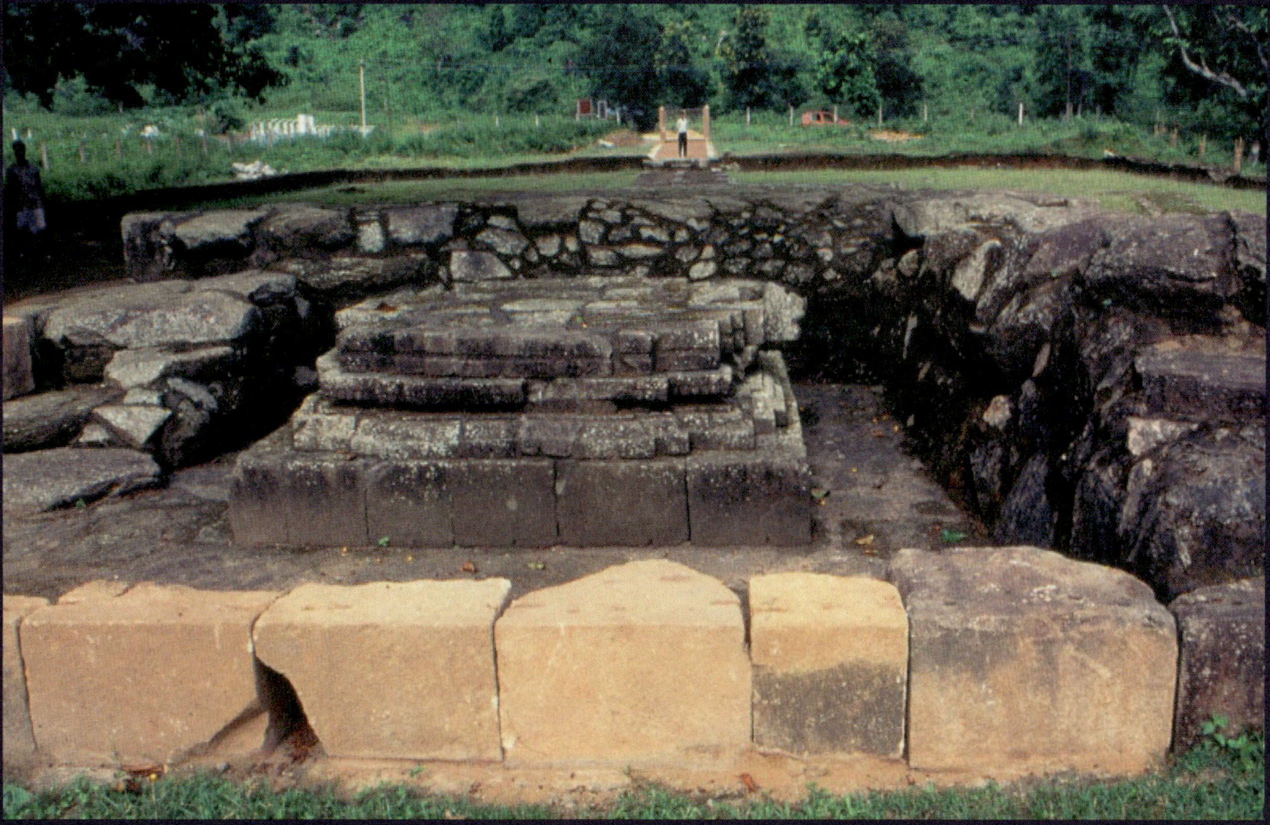

Surya Pahar

assam,the Golden Valley.

82

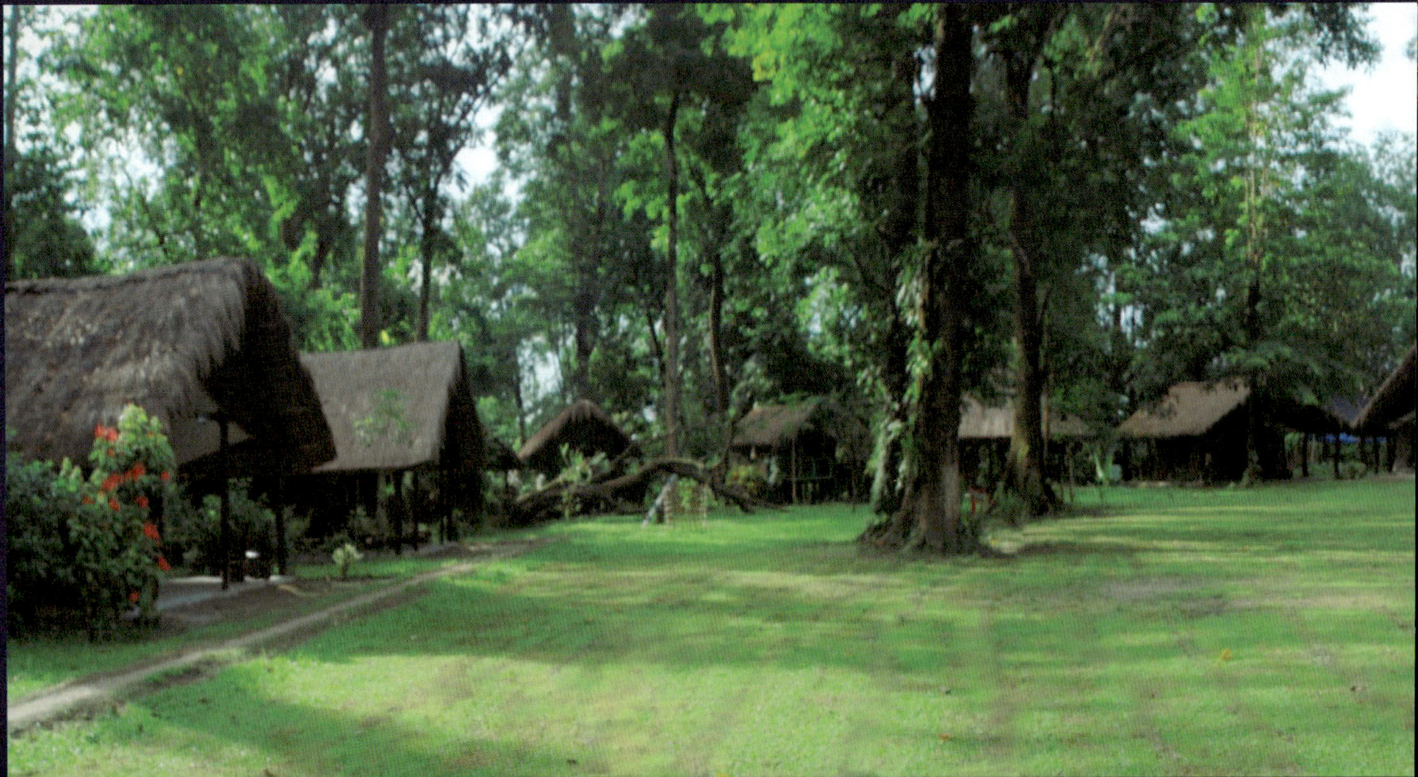

Eco Camp
at the Nameri Forest

The Eco Camp in the Nameri forest close to the border of Arunachal Pradesh at Bhalukpong is an experience. All conveniences are avail able inthis tented resort with very knwledgeable staff. One can even take an incursion into Arunachal Pracdesh Orchid reserch station at Tipi and see hundreads of varieties of Orchids
It offers you fishing, river rafting, wildlife walks and also safaris. Only suggestion is to book in advance as it is always overbooked.
The Service, food and facalities are excellent.
It is about 4 hours drive from Guhati or one hour from Tezpur.

Eco Camp

Eco Camp Facilities

86

Bhalukpong
Fishing & Watersports

Settled on the border of Assam and Arunachal Pradesh is Bhalukpung, a town shared by both the states, along the river Jia Bhorali or Kameng, as it is named in Arunachal.

The countryside is beautiful with the town spread along the river as it gushes down to the plains from the hills of Bomdila.

It is an ideal place for fishing and river rafting whenever the weather permits, after the month of September all through the winter. The rapids are probably of the 2nd or 3rd degree hence one can safely have a family outing.

Please ensure that the professionals are qualified and certified and that you wear life jackets and helmets. It is a must. **Be safe than be sorry.**

Further down river you come across the **Nameri** game park. Although inadequately provided, with advance notice Elephants can be arranged for a ride through the Park. Animal sightings here are quite frequent, including the Tiger.

For the avid fishermen Bhalukpung offers an ideal spot *for* **Mahseer**, the king of sub-Himalayan rivers fish, growing upto and sometimes over 200 pounds. Besides the local lures you can safely use golden spinners and selected plugs. Please make sure you have adequate sunlight before you cast. The local fishermen will tell you the favorite spots.

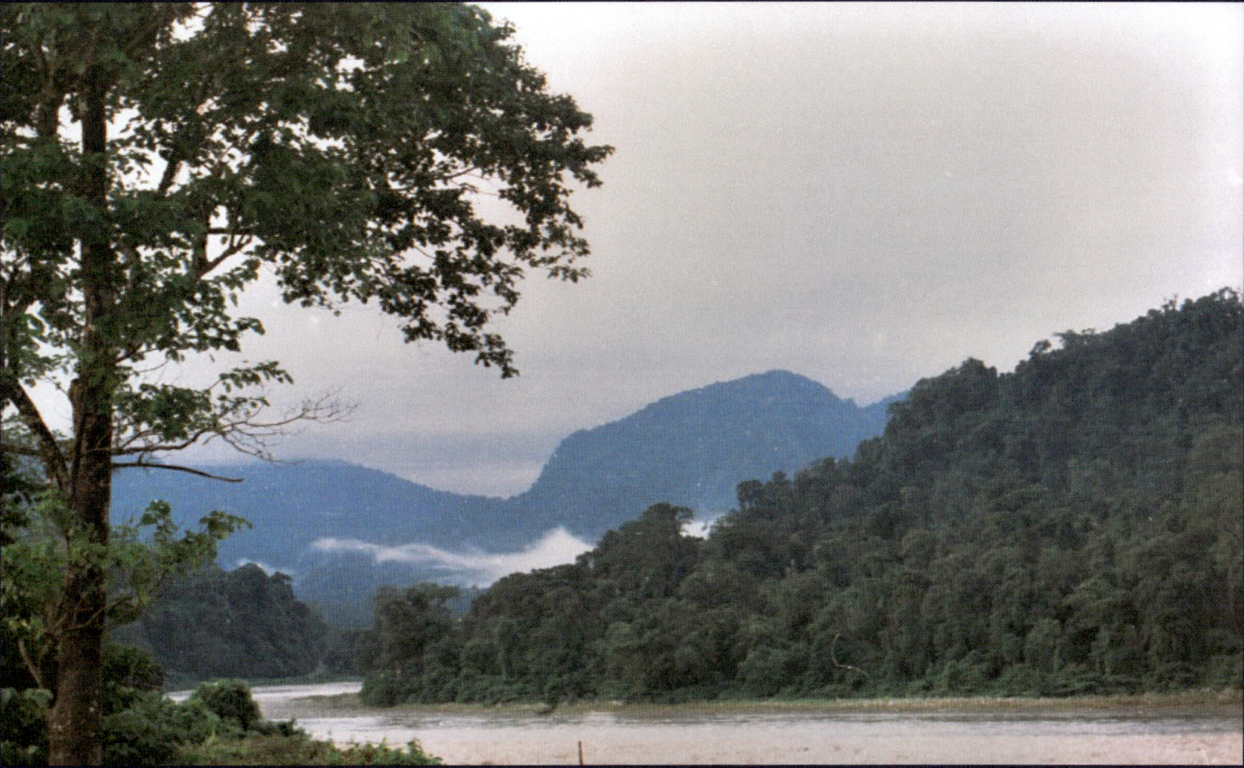

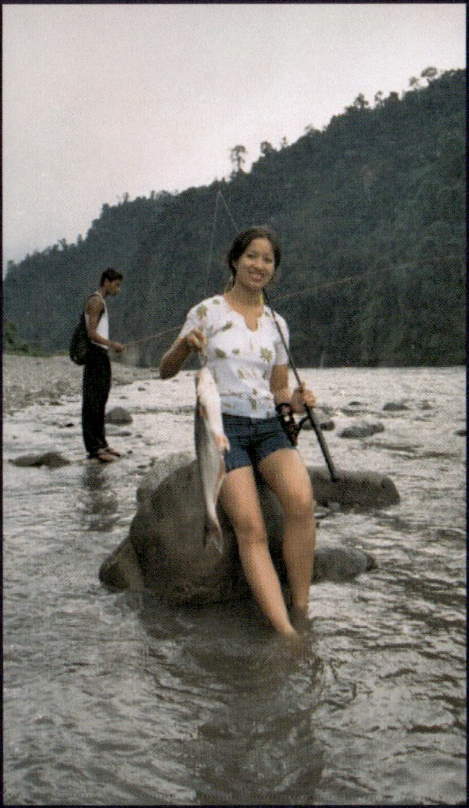

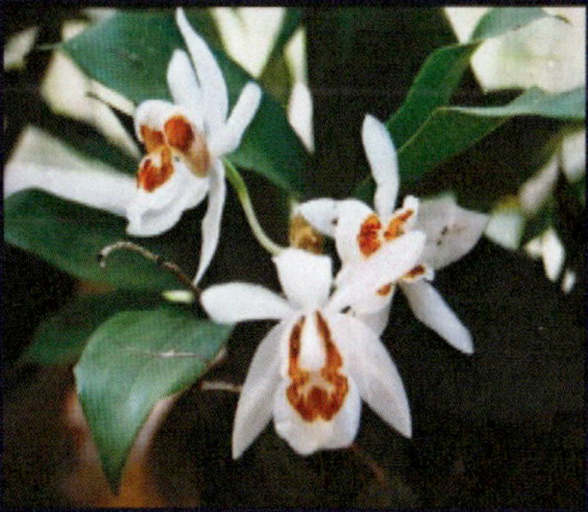

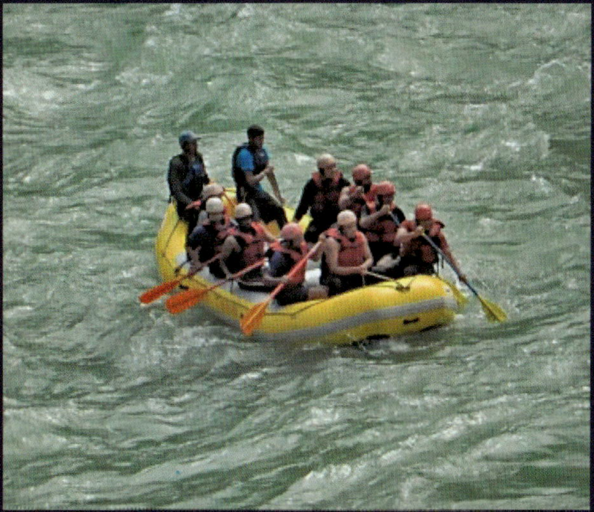

Tezpur

Legend relate that the original name of this place was 'Sonitpur' ("sonit" in Sanskrit also means blood!) or the present day name which is Tez(Blood)pur. When the battle between Lord Krishna's army and Banasura's army fought for the rescue of Aniruddha the grandson of Lord Krishna, there was so much blood shed that the whole place was stained in red. This led to the place being named Tezpur.

Historical ruins of 8th-9th century abound.The ruins of Bamuni Hills among them are the most famous, as the sculptures here resemble those of the Gupta period The ruins of Da Parbatia is a shining example of the architecture around the 4th Century AD.

Modern Tezpur was founded by the British colonial administration in 1835 as the headquarters of Darrang district.

It is one of the most important towns in the North bank as also the starting point for journeys into Arunachal Pradesh; Tawang, Itanagar, Ziro. The new bridge also connects it with other parts of Upper Assam via Nowgong.

assam,the Golden Valley.

Da Parbatia Columns

Over a 100 year School

assam, the Golden Valley.

Circuit House

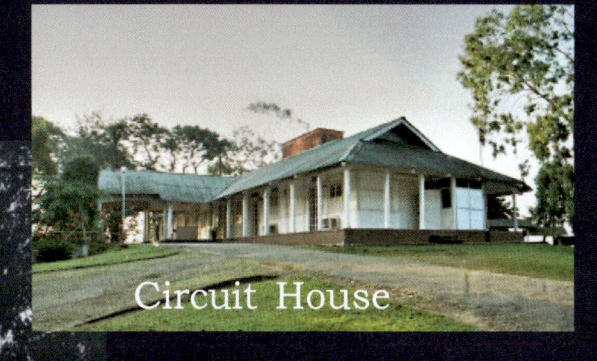

1962 War memorial

assam, the Golden Valley.

Malinithan, situated at Likaball, within about a kilometer from Balipara on the Arunachal border are ruins of a big temple belonging to 14th - 15th century. The ruins include sculptures of *Indra, Airavata, Surya and Nandi*, the Bull. Beautifully designed and decorated foundations of a temple, divine images, icon of deities, animal motifs and floral designs, carved columns and panels. The place is associated with the legend of Lord Krishna. It is believed that on the way to Dwarka from Bhismakanagar, Krishna and Rukmini were resting here and they were offered beautiful flowers by Parvati. Krishna was all praise for Parvati and addressed her as Malini-the garlandmaiden, since then the place has been known as Malinithan

assam, the Golden Valley.

Kaziranga
The home of the One Horned Rhino

Kaziranga has a history of its own. Lady Curzon first heard about the Rhinos of Kaziranga from her British tea planter friends and came to Assam in 1904-05. Although she could not see the animal, she spotted hoof prints with three toes and believed that such an animal did exist. On her return, she persuaded lord Curzon to do something to save this animal from total annihilation.

Lord Curzon set the wheels of the British bureaucracy rolling, and on June 1,1905, a preliminary notification announcing the intention of the Government to declare 57,273.60 acres of Kaziranga as a reserved forest was issued. Finally, Kaziranga was declared as reserved forest on January 3, 1908, and was officially closed for shooting.
On January 28, 1913 the area of reserved forest was expanded with the inclusion of another 13,506 acres. Kaziranga was declared a Game Sanctuary on November10, 1916.
in 1938, the then conservator of forest, A.J.W. Milroy stopped all poaching and opened Kaziranga to visitors.
Mr P D Stracey, changed the term to 'wildlife Sanctuary as the word 'game' normally referred to hunting.
Gradually the sanctuary expanded to its present sizeand finally on February 11, 1974, the name was changed to Kaziranga National Park.

The one horned Rhinoceros, Elephant, Indian bison, Swamp Deer, Samber, Hog Deer, Sloth Bear, Tiger, Leopard cat, Jungle cat, Hog badger, Capped langur, Hollock gibbon, Jackal, Goose, Hornbills, Ibis, Cormorants, Egret, Heron fishing eagle all form a part of the very complex ecological balance of the park. During Winter a large number of migratory birds flock here.
Kaziranga is 239 km from the Guwahati airport and 97 km from the Jorhat airport.It is probably the most visited destination in the Northeast.The sanctuary is divided into three divisionsKohora,Bagori and Agartoli, so three outings are a must.
The Park is open from the month of November through April.
It is 240 Kilometres from Guwahati an easy drive of about 4 hours.
The Recommended places to stay are
'Wild Grass'
'Aranya'
Day & Night bus services are available.

assam,the Golden Valley.

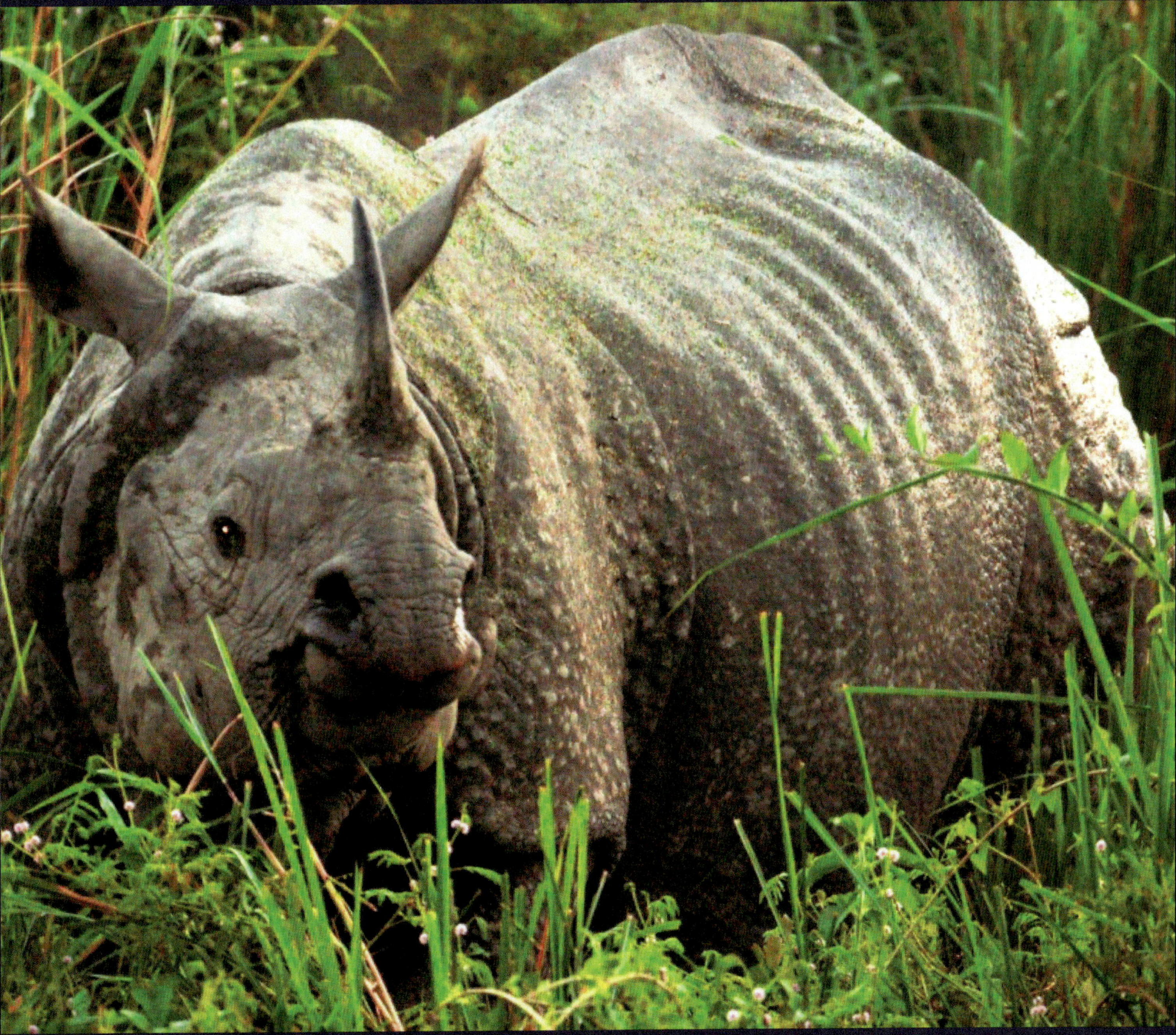

assam, the Golden Valley.

100

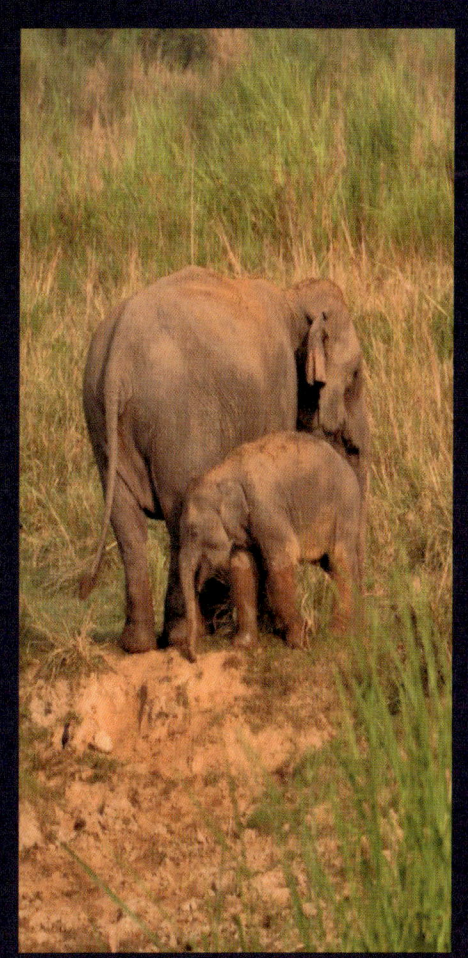

Dhekiakhowa Namghar

Dhekiakhowa needs mentioned as it is considred a *Namghar*, where one's prayers are answered more often than not.It is near Jorhat, which is one of the major Tea towns of Assam, with the Tea Reasearch Institute based at Toklai.
It is located on the highway and very convenient to find near Jorhat.

assam,the Golden Valley.

102

Dibrugarh

Dibrugarh is the metropolis for upper Assam. It is still an important city for the neighboring states and centre of all the trade of the area. In recent years it promotes Tea tourism, givng people an experience of the colonial lifestyles of the Tea planter of yester years. You can spend a fewcdays in the Tea bunglows, visit Tea gardens and factories and the colonial clubs of the area; also offers Golf for the enthusiast.

Colonial Tea Bunglows

assam, the Golden Valley.

104

Bordumsa

Budh Vihar

Buddhist Monuments

In the Margherita,Tisukia areas bordering Arunachal are many Buddhist settlements with their local monuments and worshipping temples. People who have migrated from Myanmar and as far as Yunnan in China,who still maintain their cultural practices.Cultural exchanges with their originating homelands are prevalent.In the recent years states of Assam and Arunachal Pradesh hold annual combined festivals where people from Yunnan,Myanmar and sometimes Thailand are invited..Celebrations are normally held at Pangsau pass on the Myannamar border.

assam, the Golden Valley.

Haflong
A hill-station in Karbi Along

Haflong is the only eastablished hill-station in Assam.It has a bracing climate throughout the yea; beautiful and quaint.It is again getting renouned as the Railways run a Steam Engine special from Lumding to Haflong for some of the tourist visiting Jatinga.

Circuit House

Haflong Lake

assam, the Golden Valley.

Jatinga

This is the watch tower for the enthusiasts who come to observe the annual suicide by the birds on a weekend in the Autumn. An enigma yet unexplained. On a particular night every year the birds come and dash themselves against any light they see, even if it kills them

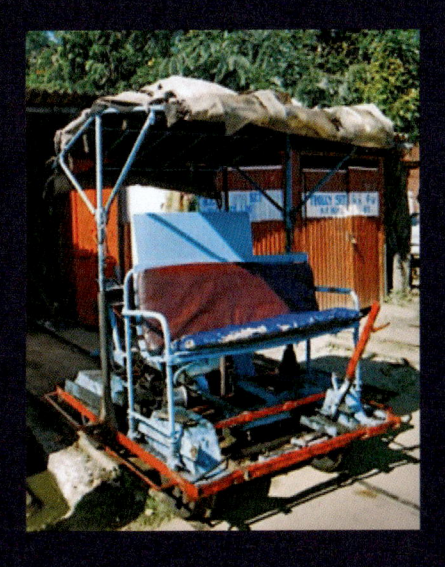

Dimasa Kingdom Ruins

assam, the Golden Valley.

Silchar

Sichar is the main city on the river Barak valley, known for its agriculture produce. It is also the centre for trade with Bangladesh, Myanmar and the neighbouring states

Barak Valley

Digboi

Digboi is the first Oil town of India.The First well dug in the 1890's is still running.Very colonial lifestyle,it offers a beautiful Golf Club and laid back holiday.

Digboi Club

assam,the Golden Valley

Ledo is the last Railway station in Assam. From here one proceeds to the Pangsau Pass, the beginning of the famous Stilwell Road to Burma.

The easternmost Railway Station

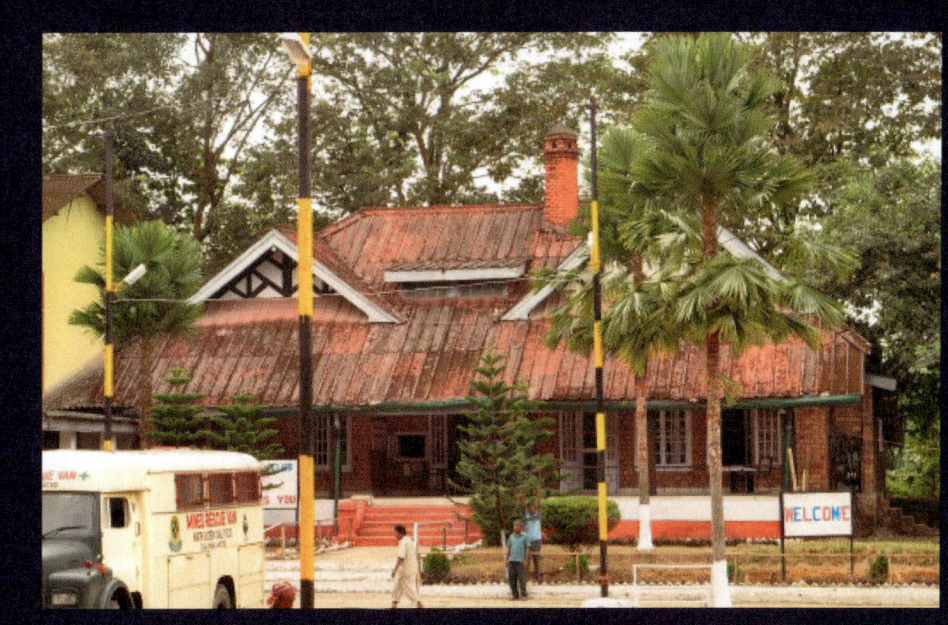

Lido Club

Wildlife Parks and Sanctuaries:

National Parks:
KAZIRANGA NATIONAL PARK

MANAS NATIONAL PARK

DIBRU-SAIKHOWA NATIONAL PARK

NAMERI NATIONAL PARK

ORANG NATIONAL PARK

Wildlife Sanctuaries:
BURA-CHAPORI WILDLIFE SANCTUARY

LAOKHOWA WILDLIFE SANCTUARY

SONAI RUPAI WILDLIFE SANCTUARY

CHAKRASHILA WILDLIFE SANCTUARY

BORNADI WILDLIFE SANCTUARY

GARAMPANI WILDLIFE SANCTUARY

PANI DIHING BIRD SANCTUARY

DEEPORBEEL BIRD SANCTUARY

BORDOIDUM BEELMUKH BIRD SANCTUARY

NAMBOR WILDLIFE SANCTUARY

Reserved Forests:

Holongpar in Jorhat District.

Jaipur in Dibrugarh District.

Barail in North Cachar District.

Dhansiri in Karbi-Anglong District.

Dumduma in Tinsukia District.

Dipu-Chirang in Kokrajhar District.

Game Safari

Kaziranga

It is the oldest National Park In Assam based in the Golaghat district covering an area of 430 Sq. Kms.

Sighting:
The one horned Rhinoceros, Elephant, Indian bison, Swamp Deer, Samber, Hog Deer, Sloth Bear, Tiger, Leopard cat, Jungle cat, Hog badger, Capped langur, Hollock gibbon, Jackal, Goose, Hornbills, Ibis, Cormorants, Egret, Heron fishing eagle etc. all form a part of the very complex ecological balance of the park. During Winter a large number of migratory birds are also seen here. The Park can be visited by Jeep, Car or on Elephant back.

Manas

It is the only Tiger Project in India .Situated in the Barpeta District It covers an area of 519.77 Sqs.

Sightings.

Hispid Hare,Pigmy Hog, Golden Langur, Indian Rhinoceros, Asiatic Buffalo etc. Other commonly seen animals are Elephant, Leopard, Clouded Leopard, Himalayan Bear, Wild Boar, Samber, Swamp Deer, Hog Deer.Jeep and Elephant Safaris are available.

Dibru Saikhowa National Park

It is situated between the Dibrugar and the Tinsukia district of eastern Assam

Sightings.

Famous for its horses and the wood ducks.It has also Hispid Hare, Pigmy Hog, Golden Langur, Indian Rhinoceros, Asiatic Buffalo etc. Other commonly seen animals are Elephant, Leopard, Clouded Leopard, Himalayan Bear, Wild Boar, Samber, Swamp Deer, Hog DeerThe best time to visit is between October and March.

Nameri National Park

Situated at the foot hills of eastern Himalayas, Nameri National Park covers an area of about 200 sq. km. It Has a backdrop of the Eastern Himalayas situated within deciduous forests and the river Jia Bhoroli runs through the park.It is about 35 km. from Tezpur town.

Jeep Safari

Tiger, Elephant, Leopard, Indian Bison, Sloth Bear, Himalayan Black Bear, Pangolin, Indian Wild Dog, Civet Cat, Capped Langur etc.

Nameri is a haven for bird watchers which include the endangered White Winged Wood duck, four species of Hornbill in abundance, the small and beautiful Scarlet Minivet, to name a few. Many species of reptiles are also found in this National Park. It is an entomologist's paradise. A huge variety of different butterflies and moths are found here. Atlas Moth with a wing span of more than 10 inches has also been spotted here.

The best season to visit is from October to April.

Orang National Park

Covering an area of 78.81 sq. kms. and is situated in the Darrang District of Assam. The animals seen in this sanctuary are the One-horned Rhinoceros, Leopard, Elephant, Sambar, Barking Deer, Tiger, varieties of water birds, Green Pigeon, Florican, Teal ,Goose. Various species of birds such as the Pelican, Cormorant, Greylag Goose, Large Whistling Teal,Great Adjutant Stork, King Vulture are also found. It is 31 Kms from Tezpur.

Pobitora Wildlife Sanctuary

Situated in the Morigaon district, Pobitora is one of the major wildlife sanctuaries of Assam. It is about 60 km. from Guwahati City, situated on the border of Nagaon and Kamrup Dist. Covering an area of 38.8 Sq. km., Pobitora is mainly famous for its Great Indian One-horned Rhinoceros. Other animals such as the Asiatic Buffalo, Leopard, Wild Bear, Civet Cat etc. are also found here. More than 200 birds and various reptiles are found in this sanctuary.

The best season to visit is from November to March.

Bura-Chapori Wildlife Sanctuary

Another magnificent wildlife sanctuary covering an area of 44.06 sq. kms, is Bura-Chapori. It is situated on the north bank of the river Brahmaputra in Sonitpur District.It is considered to be an ideal habitat for the Bengal Florican.Various species of migratory birds are also seen here.Other attractions are the Great Indian One horned Rhinoceros, Asiatic Buffalo, Wild Boar, Otter, Civet Cat, Leopard Cat, Barking Deer, etc. Various reptiles and fish are also found here

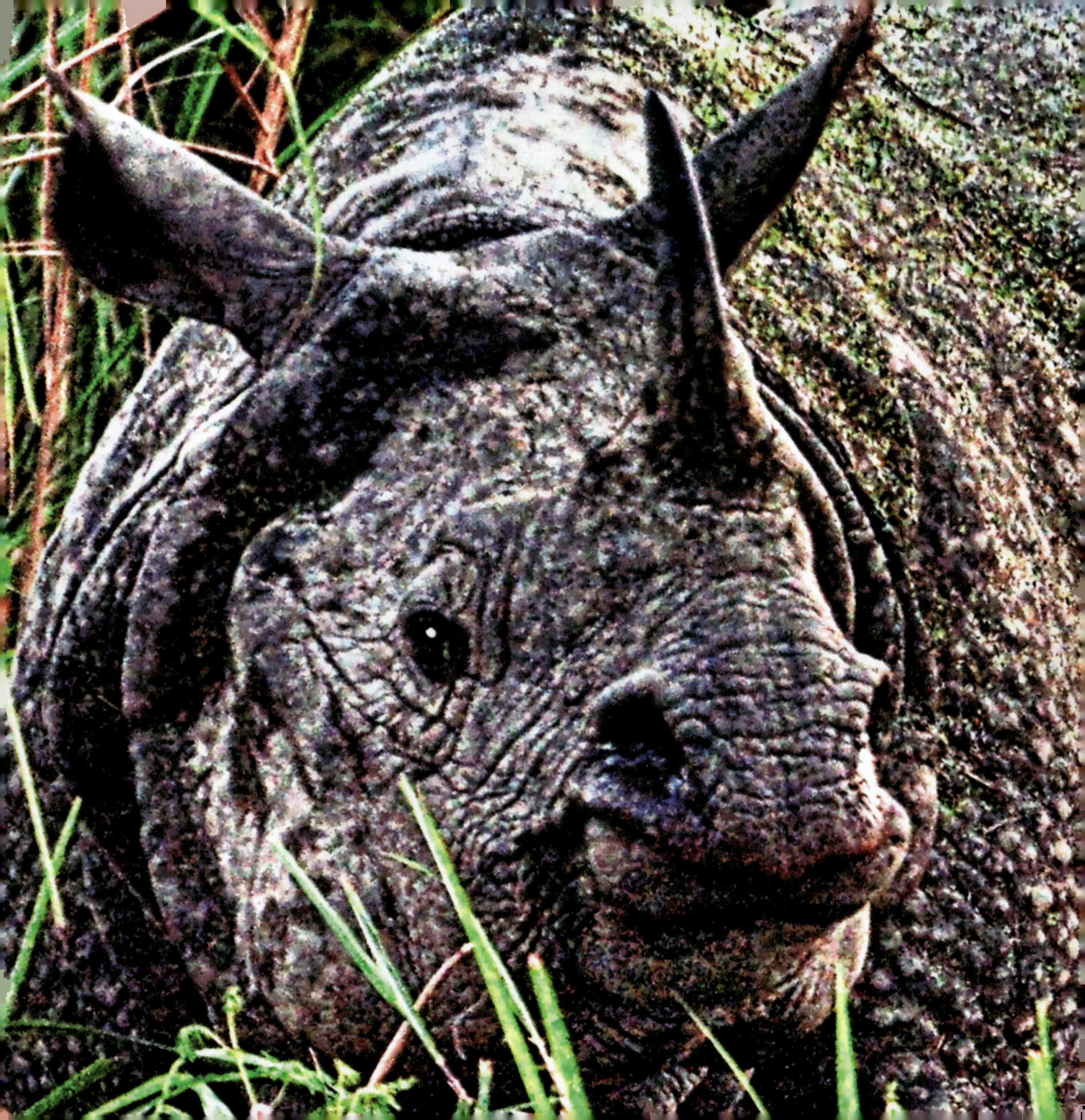

Laokhowa Wildlife Sanctuary

Covering an area of 70.13 sq. kms Laokhowa Wildlife Sanctuary is situated in Nagaon Dist. and is only 25 kms from Nagaon town. Its main attraction is the Great Indian one horned Rhinocerous. Other animals found here are Tiger, Elephant, Leopard, Asiatic Buffalo, Wild Boar, Civet Cat, Leopard Cat, Hog Deer etc. Various species of birds and reptiles are also found in Laokhowa.

Sonai Rupai Wildlife Sanctuary

This wildlife sanctuary, 220 Sq. Kms. in area, is situated in Sonitpur District. Extending along the Himalayan foothills it offers a magnificent view of both scenery and wildlife. The sanctuary is home to Elephants, Indian Bison, Deer and a variety of hill birds.

Chakrashila Wildlife Sanctuary

Covering an area of approximately 45.568 sq. kms, this sanctuary is located in the Dhubri District of Assam and is 68 kms from Dhubri. It is surrounded by hills and there are two lakes on either side of the sanctuary. The world famous Golden Langur was discovered here in the year 1986.

Many different mammals, birds, twenty three species of reptiles, more than forty butterfly species are found in this area. Hornbills are also seen here.

Bornadi Wildlife Sanctuary

Wedged between the Himalayas and Bhutan, this sanctuary is situated in the Darrang District of Assam. It covers an area of 26.22 sq kms. It was declared a wildlife sanctuary especially for the protection of the Hispid Hare and Pigmy Hog.

Garampani Wildlife Sanctuary

This small sanctuary, covering an area of 6.05 sq. kms. is Situated in Karbi Anglong district, it is 25 kms from Golaghat and 65 kms from Kaziranga National Park. This area is famous for its hot water springs.

Animals found here are Elephants, Leopards,Tigers, Deer, Golden Langurs, Hoolok Gibbons in additon to a large variety of birds and reptiles.

122

Pani Dihing Bird Sanctuary

It covers an area of 33.93 sq. kms, It is situated in Sibsagar district. Pani Dihing is famous for migratory birds. Adjutant Storks, Fishing Eagle are commonly found here.

Deeporbeel Bird Sanctuary

Deeporbeel is situated at a distance of 18 kms from Guwahati city In this area 120 different types of birds have been listed by Dept of Forest, Assam. Adjutant Storks, Fishing Eagle, Kingfisher are found here.

Bordoibum Beelmukh Bird Sanctuary

Bordoibum Beelmukh is a Bird sanctuary. It is situated at 50-55 metres above sea level in Dhemaji district. Bordoibam was formed after the great earthquake of 1950 when the river Subansiri changed its course. Adjutant Storks, Fishing Eagle are found here.

Nambor Wildlife Sanctuary

Nambor Wildlife Sanctuary covers an area of 37 sq. kms. Situated in Karbi Anglong district. It is 25 kms from Golaghat and 65 kms from Kaziranga National Park. Animals commonly found here are Elephants, Tigers and Leapords.

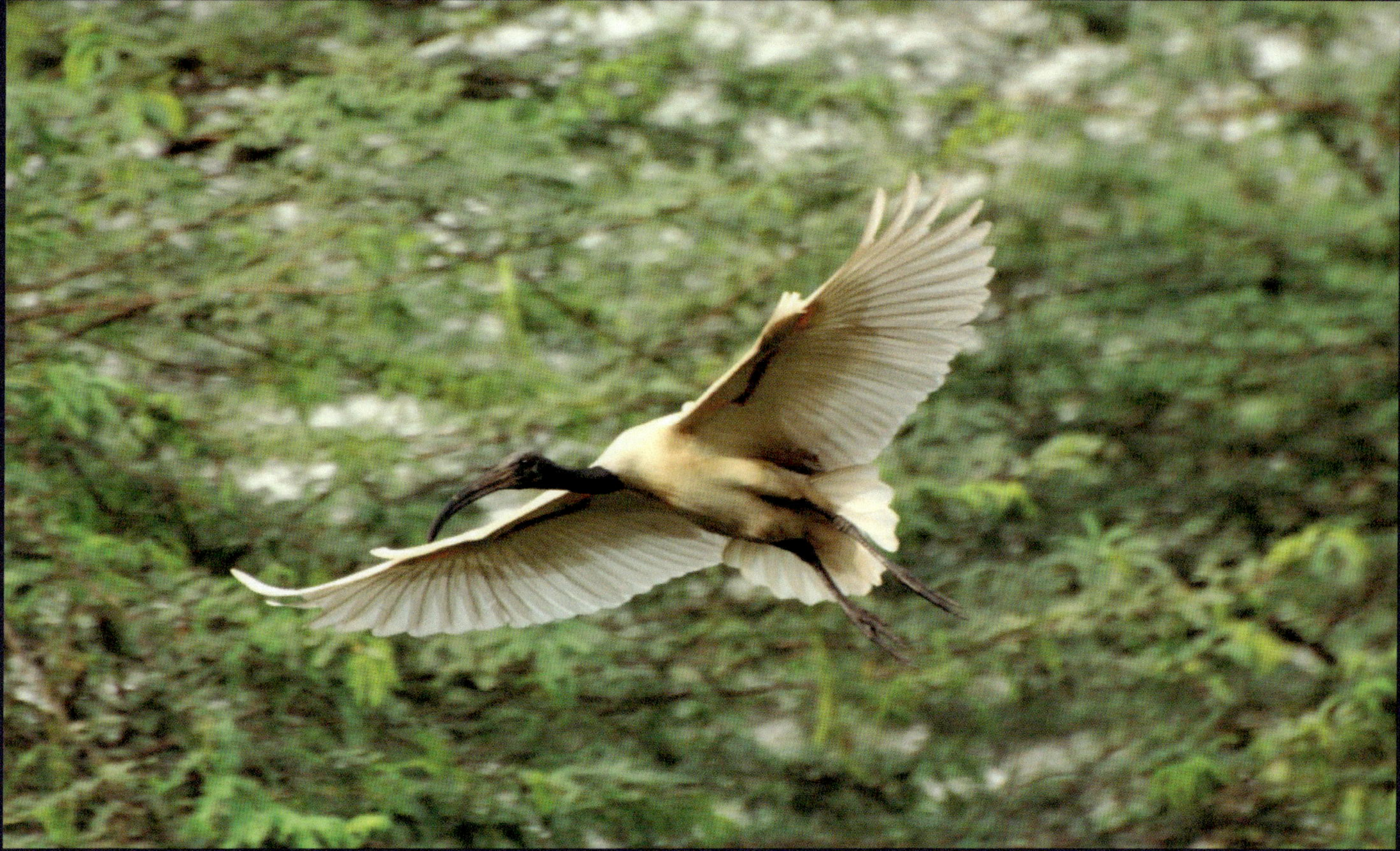

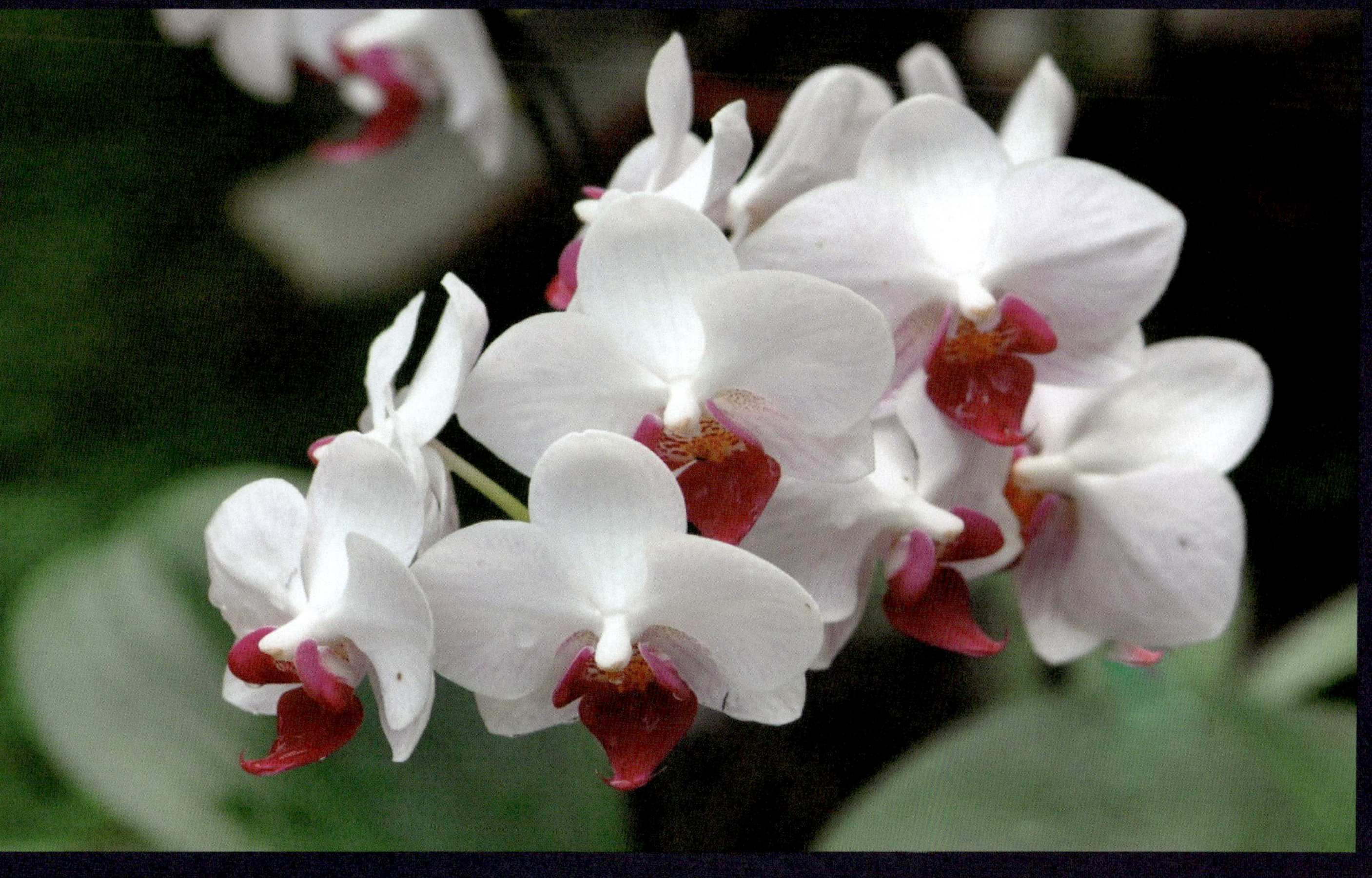

Important Festivals of Assam

Assam is a part of the **Rice culture** which extends from Xian in China to the banks of the *Padma* in Bangladesh. Today most of the rice is grown by the wet process and hence significantly depended on the weather, which, at the advent of history, was ordained.

All the festivals are, in some form or the other, related to the sowing or cropping of the golden grain. There are festivals and rituals to pray for good weather and bountiful crops followed by thanksgiving once the crop is cut and stored.

Bihu

Bihu is the most important festival of Assam, celebrated by all the Assamese people irrespective of class and creed .In a year Bihu is celebrated on three occasions. During Bihu Assam becomes a riot of color and celebrations with cultural performances in every village, town and city of the state.

Bohag Bihu which augurs good harvest at the time of sowing celebrated on the 14th of April every year, **Kaati Bihu** which is observed to mark the cutting and binding of grains and **Magh Bihu** at the onset of harvesting celebrated on the 14th of January annually..

Ambubachi Mela

Held in Mid June during the monsoon it is a very important festival of the **Shakti** cult. Kamakhya Temple in Guwahati has been a center for **Tantra** and *Shakti* worship for centuries. Many *Tantra* rituals are performed during the festival which lasts for a fortnight. *Shakti* and *Tantra* believers arrive here from many parts of India, Nepal and Bangladesh on the occasion.

This is believed to be the period during which the Godess **Kamakhya** has her annual menstrual cycle. The temple doors close for the first three days, and when they finally open it is believed, to be a new beginning for the Earth and its people.

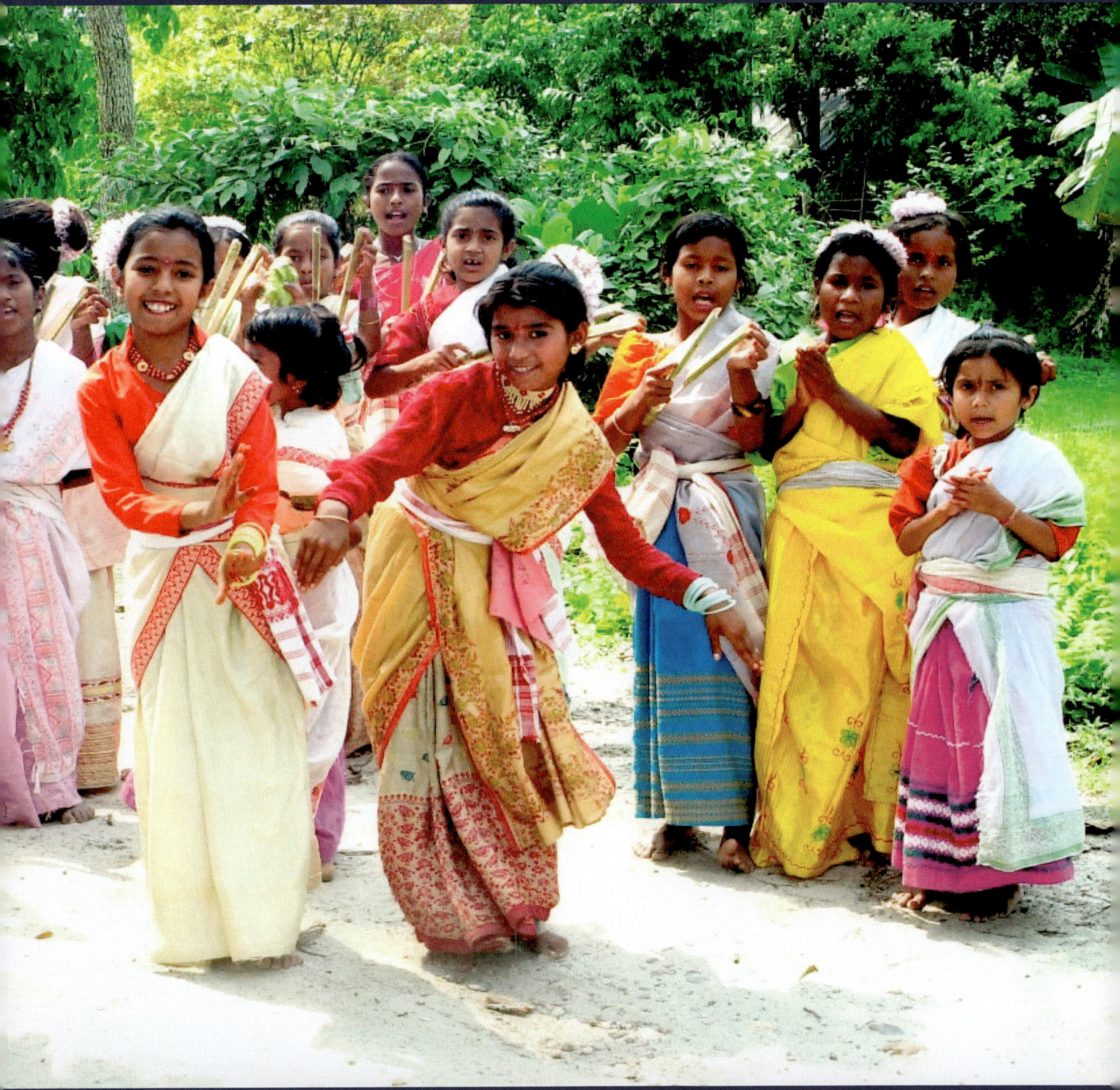

Me-Dum-Me-Phi.

This is the festival of Ancestral worship; the concept of filial piety. Held on the 31st of January, the Ahom brethren get together at a selected location in their traditional finery and celebrate with their family and friends.

Baishagu

'Baishagu' is generally celebrated by the Bodo Kacharis during mid April. It is the most important of the Bodo tribe .It coincides with the Bihu festival which is celebrated at the advent of the New Year,14th April.

On the eve of the festival, the cow is worshipped. The next day which is the first day of the month of Bohag in the Assamese calendar the young exchange visits to pay obeisance to the elders in the family. Lord Shiva known as *Bathou*, is worshipped and offered chicken and rice beer ritually for the well being of the community.

There is merriment and dancing among all accompanied by musical instruments indigenously developed; *Khum*, the drum,*Jotha* the manjari, *Khawbang*,the cymbals, *Gogona*, the mouth organ and *siphung* the flute.

At the end of the celebrations the people get together at *Garjasali*, a place for community worship

Bohaggiyo Bishu

This is the most important festival of the Deoris of Assam. The term 'Bi' means extreme and 'Su' means 'rejoicing' which like the theme of all the springtime festivals of the valley.

However unlike the other communities, the Bahaggiyo Bishu not necessarily falls on the 14th of January, as the day of starting the festival as on the eve of the festival *Than Puja* is offered which is customarily on a Wednesday. Once in every four years a white buffalo is sacrificed for appeasement of the Gods, which actually is a substitute for a traditional human sacrifice. During the festival *Deodhani* dance is performed and various compositions of the *Hussori*, a form of carol, is sung.

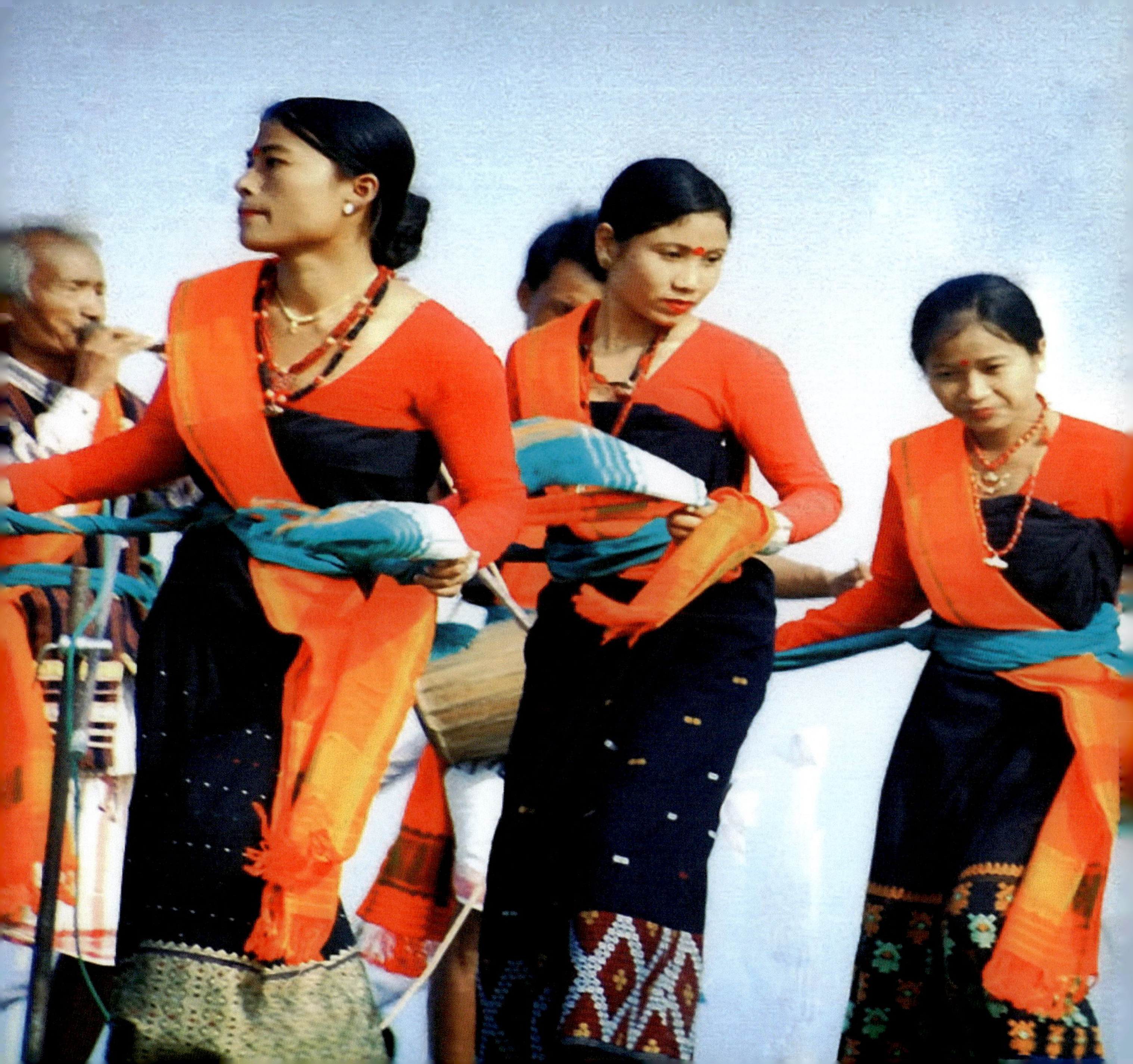

Dosa Thoi! Long Nai

This is a religious dance performed at the 'Bathou Puja' or worshipping of Lord Shiva. In this dance the priestess called Deodini dances with a bowl of blood of a sacrificed fowl on her head. It is believed that during the performance the dancer goes into a trance, during which Bathou or Lord Shiva appears and drinks the blood in the bowl.

Rajini Gabra & Harni Gabra

It is the annual festival of the Dimasa people, held before the starting of the cultivation season tribe. Rajini Gabra is celebrated during day time. The 'Kunang' or the headman of the village closes the village gates and then the ceremony starts by propitiating the family. On the same night 'Harni Gabra' is performed for the protection and well being of the family.
If during the ritual any outsider enter the premises, it is considered ill and the outsider has to pay for the ceremonies as a penalty for the intrusion.

Rongker and Chomangkan

Rongker and Chomangkan are festivals of the Karbis, It is a springtime festival celebrated at the beginning of the Assamese New Year. 14th April. Rituals are performed to propitiate the Gods and Goddesses for the well being of the people in the coming year. It is organized by the elder men folk and women are seldom permitted in the ritual area. It is a ritualistic festival for the well being of the clan and a disease free bountiful harvest for the community. On the other hand, *Chomangkan* is the festival of filial piety. It is a ritual performed for the well being of the forefathers. There are no fixed dates and the elders can decide the same in consultation with the entire community. The celebrations last for 4 days and 4 nights.

130

Ali-Ai-Ligang

It is probably one of the most colorful festival of Assam celebrated by the Mishing people. It is held on the first Wednesday (*Ligange lange*) of the month of *'Ginmur Polo'* (February-March). *'Ali'* means root, seed; *'Ai'* means fruit and *'Ligang'* means sow. The sowing starts on this day and it is celebrated with young boys and girls attired in their colorful best dancing to music.
It is followed by a feast of *Poro Apong*, rice beer, pork, fish and sweet delicacies. It continues for five days during which, fishing hunting, plowing is totally prohibited.
Mishing cuisine is delicious, a must to try.

Baikho

Rabha is another community of Assam is fast diminishing. It does not have any fixed days for its famous festival called *Baikho*. The individual groups fix their own dates.
Baikho this springtime festival is celebrated for propitiating the Gods for a good harvest and also the well being of the community as whole. Rituals of offering food and drinks to appease the Gods, is followed by eating, drinking and dancing in merriment.

The other organized festivals are;

Brahmaputra Beach Festival, in the middle of January

The **Rongali Utsav,** in the second half of January

The **Kaziranga festival,** sometime in February

132

Ethnic People of Assam

Deoris:

The Deoris are one of the important ethnic communities of Assam. Drawing their ancestary from the Chutias, who ruled most of the eastern parts of Assam, before the onset of the Ahom Kings. They were the community priests of the Chutias.

The Deories are divided into four clans. People living on the banks of the rivers Debong, Tengapani and Borgang belonged to the Debongia, Tengapania and Borgoya clan respectively. Those inhabiting the region of Potarohal belonged to Patargoya clanwhich has since become extinct

At present, the Deoris live in the districts of Lakhimpur, Sonitpur, Jorhat, Sivasagar, Dibrugarh, Dhemaji and in the Sadiya region of Tinsukia district. Agriculture is the mainstay of the Deoris.

The Deoris, like other communities of Assam, also celebrate the Bihu festival which they call 'Bishu". They generally observe the Magh Bihu and the Bohag Bihu. In both occasions prayers are offered and animal sacrifices are performed in the *'Thaan Ghar'*, a common place of worship. During the festivals *Huchori* and *Hurairangoli* is sung by the village maidens accompanied with clapping of hand and local musical instruments. *Deodhani* dances are performed by selected few who have been possessed. An Oracle interprets the outcome of these sacrificial dances.

Ancestral lineage is claimed from *Aobobo*, a mythical forefather.

Kachari's

The Kachari's are the third largest group in Assam, largely settled in and around the Dibrugarh district. They are followers of the *vaishnav Mahapurushia* faith propagated by Sri *Shankardev*. Culturally very rich in their folklore, the songs sung by the men are called *Geet* and the ones sung by women are called *Naam*. Most of these

134

community songs are sung in praise of God. They also have distinct dance forms called *Hugra*, *Bohuwa* and *Kula-Burhir*.

The origin of the name Kachari is indistinct but the Sonawal prefix is possibly attached to their name as they were gold panners in the rivers around Dibrugarh, Jorhat, Tinsukia and Golaghat.

The sonowal kacharis have seven clans called *Khel*. Namely; Balikhitiari, Chiripuria, Amarabamiya, Dhulial, Ujani-Kuchiya, Namoni-kuchiya and Tipamiya..

Over the years they have amalgamated into the mainstream of Assam and assumed common surnames.

Mishing

The Mishings, now called Misings are an ethnic group inhabiting the districts of Dhemaji, North Lakhimpur, Sonitpur, Tinsukia, Dibrugarh, Sibsagar, Jorhat and Golaghat. They are the smallest tribal group in North-East India. They were earlier called Miris and the Constitution of India still refers them as Miris.

Somewhere around the 13th century, they started migrating towards the plains of Assam looking for the alluvial river banks. This exodus continued for centuries.
As fate would have it, they found one of the most fertile river-bed in the whole world and settled on both banks along the length of the river, starting right from Sadiya in the east, to Jorhat in the west. They continued to live in stilted houses, known as *Chang ghar*. It was elevated against flood waters during the rainy season as well as a protection from wild beasts.
Due to the annual floods the Misings lived a life of abject poverty and misery. Agriculture being their main occupation, floods affect them in more ways than one. Morever, due to their affinity towards living close to river banks brought about Malaria and water-borne diseases. But they continue to live along the banks of the Brahmaputra and its tributaries, unfazed by the disasters.

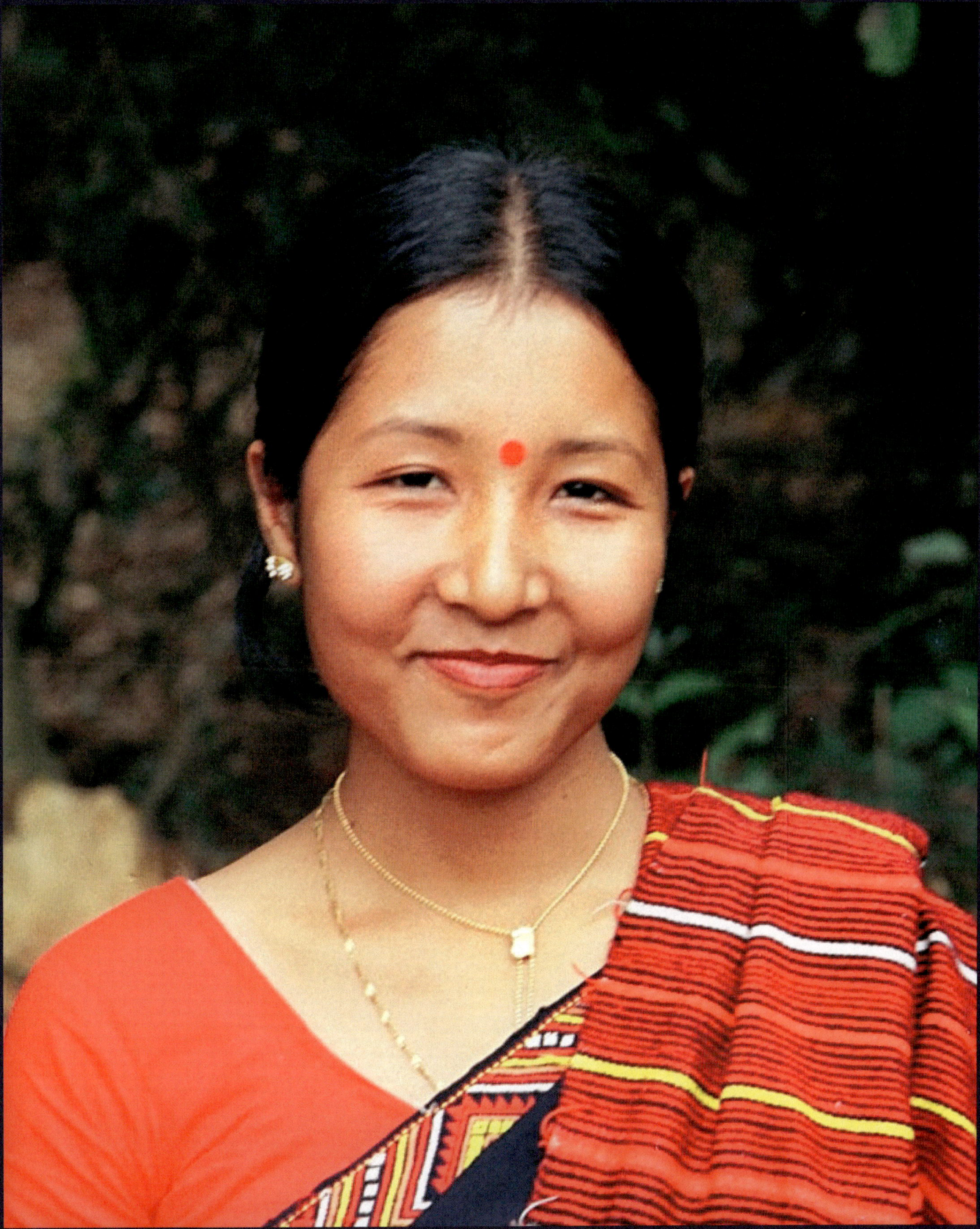

Their chief festival is Ali-Aye-Ligang, is in the month of February, which marks the beginning of the sowing season. Most Misings follow both the Donyi-Polo (Sun and Moon Worship) and Hindu religion.

The language of the Mising people is also known as Mising language. Misings are broadly divided into:

- Dagdoong (belonging to the North), and
- Daktok (belonging to the South).

Typically, it is easy to identify if a person is Dagdoong or Daktok from his surname. A further classification can be based on the "dialect" of the language. These groups are:

- Pagro,
- Moying,
- Sayang,
- Oyan, and
- Samuguri

The variations of Mising spoken by these groups differ from each other in intonation, sentence formation, word usage, with the exception of Samugurias, who do not speak Mising at all. They use Assamese instead.

Mising surnames reflect the clan they belong to. They can be divided into two main clans:

- Pegu, and
- Doley.

This is a social setup that has been followed since time immemorial. Other clans (people having surnames besides Doley and Pegu) claim brotherhood with either Pegu or Doley. For example, Patirs, Pathori and Lagachus are regarded as brothers to Pegus. Similarly, Kutums and Kulis are regarded as related to Doley.

138

This classification of "brotherhood" was made primarily for marital reasons. Clans belonging to the same brotherhood of Pegu do not marry within the clan, and the same applies for the Doley brotherhood. However, there is a group that can freely marry within either Pegu or Mili. Surnames like Morang, Payeng, Pangging,Taye, Mili belong to this group. Marriage between two people having the same surname is taboo.

Karbi

The Karbis, mentioned as the Mikir in the Constitution Order of the Government of India, are one of the major ethnic groups in North-east India and especially in the hill areas of Assam. They prefer to call themselves Karbi, and sometimes Arleng (literally "man" in the Karbi language). The term Mikir is now not preferred .The closest meaning of mikir could said to be derieved from "Mekar".

Besides Karbi Anglong district, the Karbi inhabited areas include North Cachar Hills, Kamrup, Marigaon district, Nagaon, Golaghat, Karimganj and Sonitpur districts ;Balijan circle of Papumpare district in Arunachal Pradesh, Jaintia Hills, Ri Bhoi and East Khasi Hills districts in Meghalaya and Dimapur District in Nagaland. The Karbis constitutes the third largest community in Assam after the Bodos and the Mishings

The Karbis too trace their origin and existence in China and South-east Asia. The traditional Karbi kingdom included Rongkhang, "Kiling", Amri, Chinthong, Nilip-Lumbajong and Longku-Longtar, which corresponds to the present day Hamren subdivision of Karbi Anglong district, Kamrup and Marigaon districts, eastern part of Karbi Anglong and the North Cachar Hills district.

The Karbis are a Patrilineal,society and is composed of five major clans or Kur. They are Ingti, Terang, Inghi, Teron and Timung which are again divided into many sub-clans. These clans are exogamous.The traditional system of governance is headed by the Lindok or the king, who is assisted by the Katharpo, the Dilis, the Habes and the Pinpos. These posts of administration, however, are now merely ceremonial with no real power.

assam,the Golden Valley

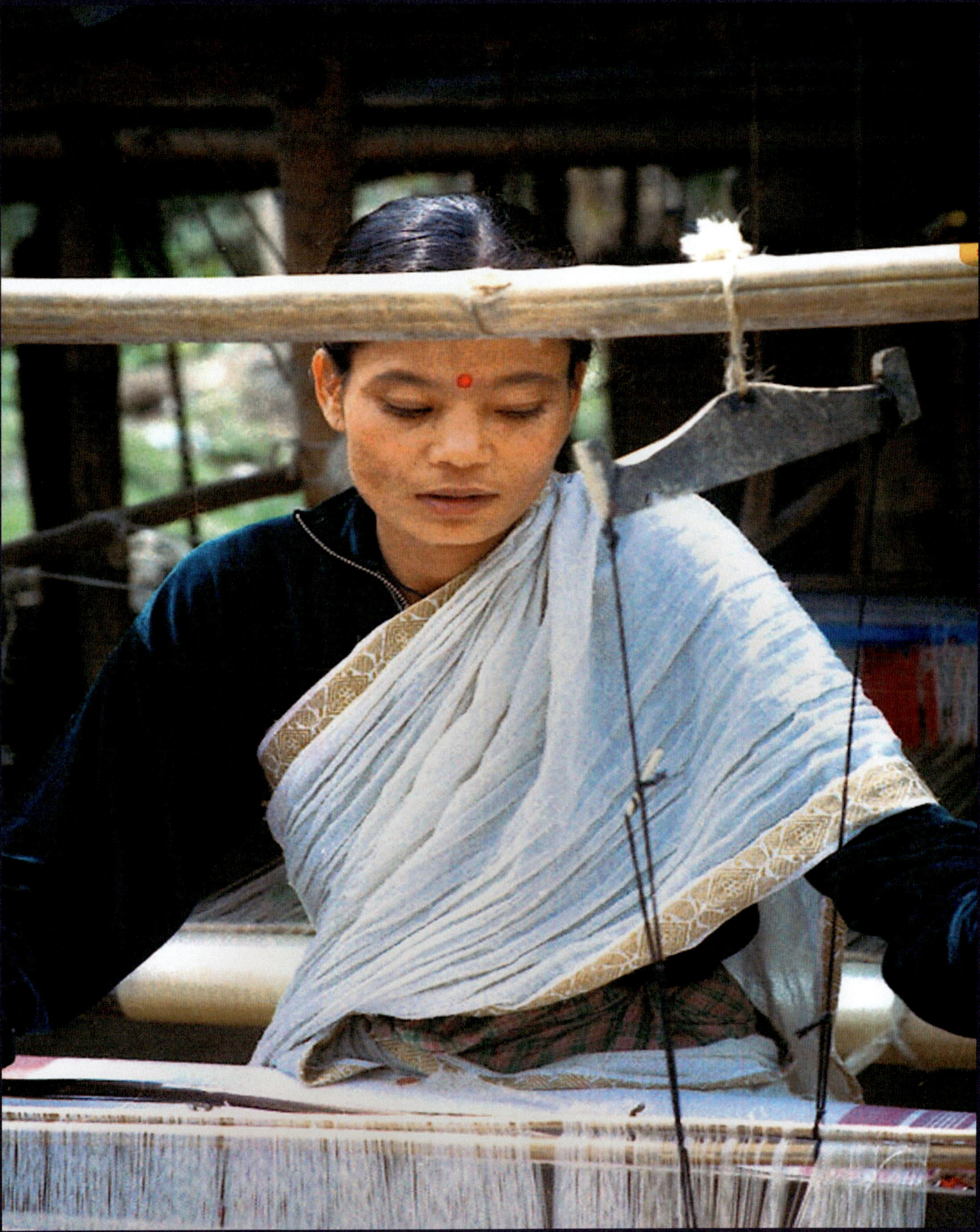

The Karbis celebrate many festivals. Rongker is one such festival held around January-February by the entire village as thanksgiving to the various gods and for the prosperity and the well-being of the community. The Chomkan (also known as "thi-karhi" and Chomangkan) is a festival unique to the Karbis. It is actually a ceremony performed by a family for the peace and the safe passage of the soul of family members who died. Most of the Karbis still practice their traditional belief system, which is animistic called Honghari in Karbi .The practitioners of Honghari believe in reincarnation and honour the ancestors, besides the traditional deities like Hemphu and Mukrang.

The Karbi women are expert weavers and they wear home-made clothes. Their main attire consist of the pekok, a piece of cloth with designs, wrapped around the uppertorso and tied into a knot on the right shoulder, the pini, similar to a sarong and a vamkok, a decorative piece of cloth tied around the waist .The men's traditional dress consist of the choi, a sleeveless shirt with a 'V' neck and with tassels at the bottom edges, a rikong, which looks like a dhoti and a poho, a turban.

The Karbis traditionally practice jhum cultivation (slash and burn cultivation) in the hills. They grow variety of crops which include grains, vegetables and fruits like rice, maize, potato, tapioca, beans, ginger and turmeric. They are quiet self-sufficient and have homestead gardens with betel nut, jackfruit, oranges, pineapple which fulfill their daily needs.

Dimasa

The Dimapur Kingdom of the thirteen-century extended along the southern bank of the Brahmaputra, from the Dikhow river in the east to Kalang in the west and Dhansiri valley. According to a Kachari tradition, the Muli bamboo(Wa-thi) flowers once after ever fifty years and during the region of the Kachari Kings at Dimapur these flowered nine times This means that they had ruled for 450 years at Dimapur, and since the Kacharis shifted their capital to Maibang in 1536 A.D Kacharis must have established Dimapur approximately in 1087 A.D.At the time of the Ahom quest, the Dimapur kingdom was at its height.

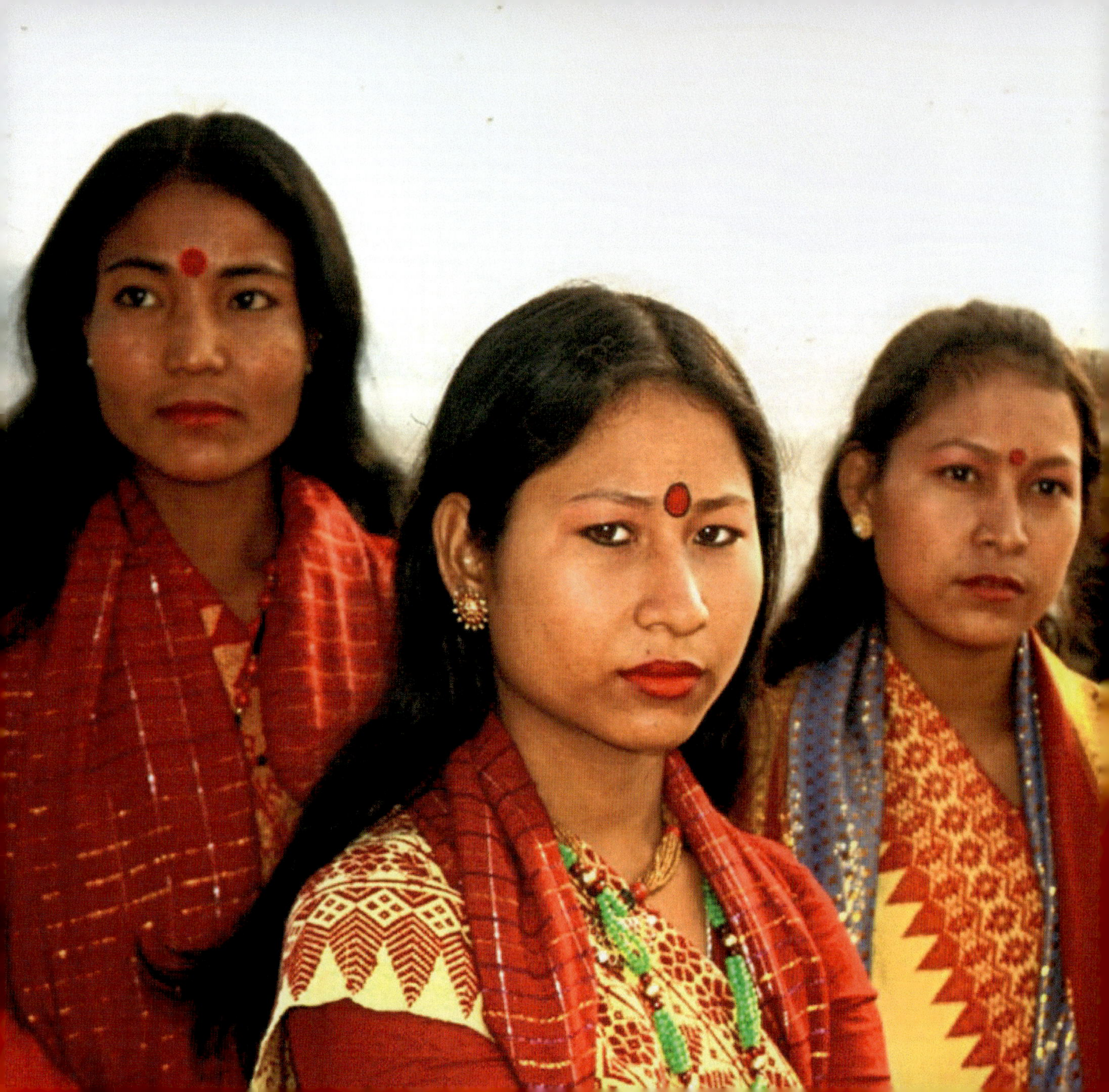

The beginning of the end of glorious Rule of the Kacharis at Dimapur began with the advent of the Ahoms in the fifteenth century. After defeating the Kacharis monarch Khunkradao Raja, the Ahoms installed Dehtsung, the kings brother, as Dimapur King on condition of allegiance to the Ahoms ruler. However, within a few years the Kachari king revolted and refused to pay tribute to the Ahoms ruler and thus another battle became inevitable and in 1536 A. D. and was fought. The Kachari King was completely defeated and the city of Dimapur was sacked. The survivors of the ruling clan along with loyal subjects thereafter shifted their capital to Maibang.

From Dimapur, the royal family of Kachari in their last lag of migration moved to Kashpur of Cachar district of Assam. The Kachari kingdom finally was annexed by the British East India co. along with Assam, following Yandabu Treaty.

Situated on the banks of the river Dhansiri, (originally known as Dang-siri meaning a ravine of peaceful habitation) Dimapur, often described as the 'Brick City' by European scholars and also by the Ahoms, was the ancient capital of a ruling nation, the Kacharis, who were once a powerful and predominant race in the Entire North-East region particularly the Brahmaputra Valley. In Ahom Chronicles Dimapur has been described as 'Che-din-chi-pen' (town-earth-burn-make) meaning 'brick town' or ' Che-Dima' meaning town of Dimasa

Rabha

The Rabhas have similarities with other members of Bodo group such as Garos, Kachari, Mech, Koch, Hajong and others Most of the Rabhas of Dooars refer to themselves as Rabha, but some of them often declare themselves as Kocha. The socio-religious and material life of the Rabhas have similarities with those of the Pani-Koch. The Rabhas of West Bengal and Assam generally speak the local Bengali and Assamese dialects. The Rabhas,

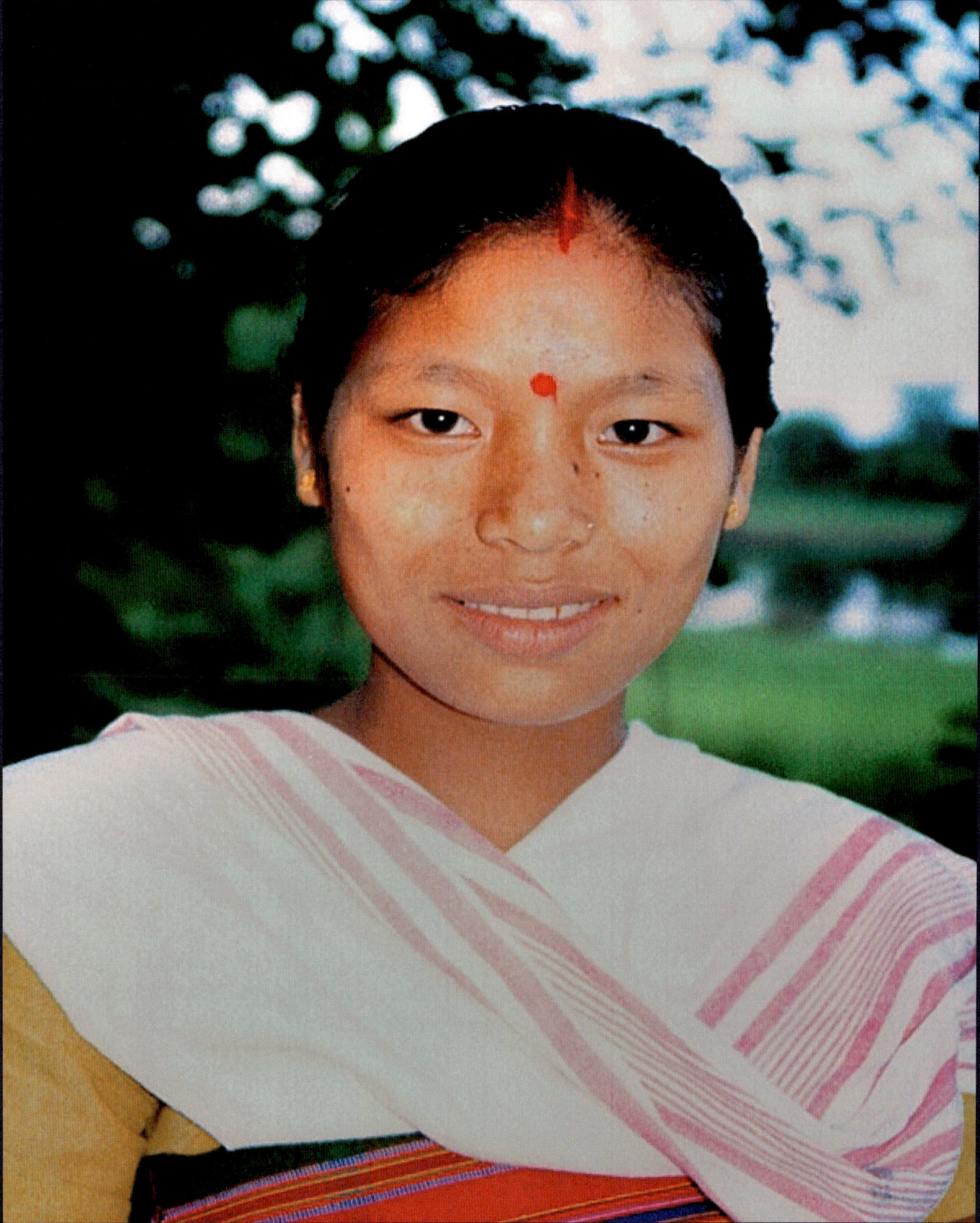

who live in the forest villages, have retained their original Rabha dialect to a great extent.

The traditional economy of the Rabhas in general, is based on agriculture, forest based activities and weaving. In the past, the Rabhas used to practice shifting cultivation. They continued to cultivate the land with Gogo or bill-hook. Later they took up the job of settled cultivation and started cultivation with plough.

Today, one finds Rabhas in diverse occupations from forest workers and cultivators to all modern occupations like school teachers and government and industry jobs.

Rabha people traditionally practice a few animistic rituals. However, today they more often follow a faith, which is a blend of some Hindu and a few animistic rituals. There are considerable differences in ritual practices among forest Rabhas who still live in the forest villages and theRabhas who have been living in the villages as cultivators. The forest Rabhas follow traditional animistic practices with some rituals of mainstream Hinduism. On the other hand village Rabhas have merged with local Hindus.

Rabha people's religious world is interwovwn with various spirits and natural objects. The main deity of the Rabhas is called Rishi. Rishi, for the forest Rabhas as well as village Rabhas, is a male deity. He is also known as Mahakal. Forest Rabhas worship him in all important social and religious ceremonies.

In addition the deities Rungtuk and Basek, represented by two earthen pots of rice placed on the northern side of the store. These two deities are considered as the daughters of Rishi or Mahakal. Rungtuk and Basek are household deities and considered as the deities of wealth like the Hindu Goddess Lakshmi. The Rungtuk and basek, are inherited by the heiress of the family. Their traditional priest deosi, calculates the auspicious day for installing these deities. The room where they are kept is occupied by the head of the family. The deities do not have any idols. A red coloured earthen pitcher filled with rice represents the deity Rungtuk. An egg is kept on the neck of this pitcher.

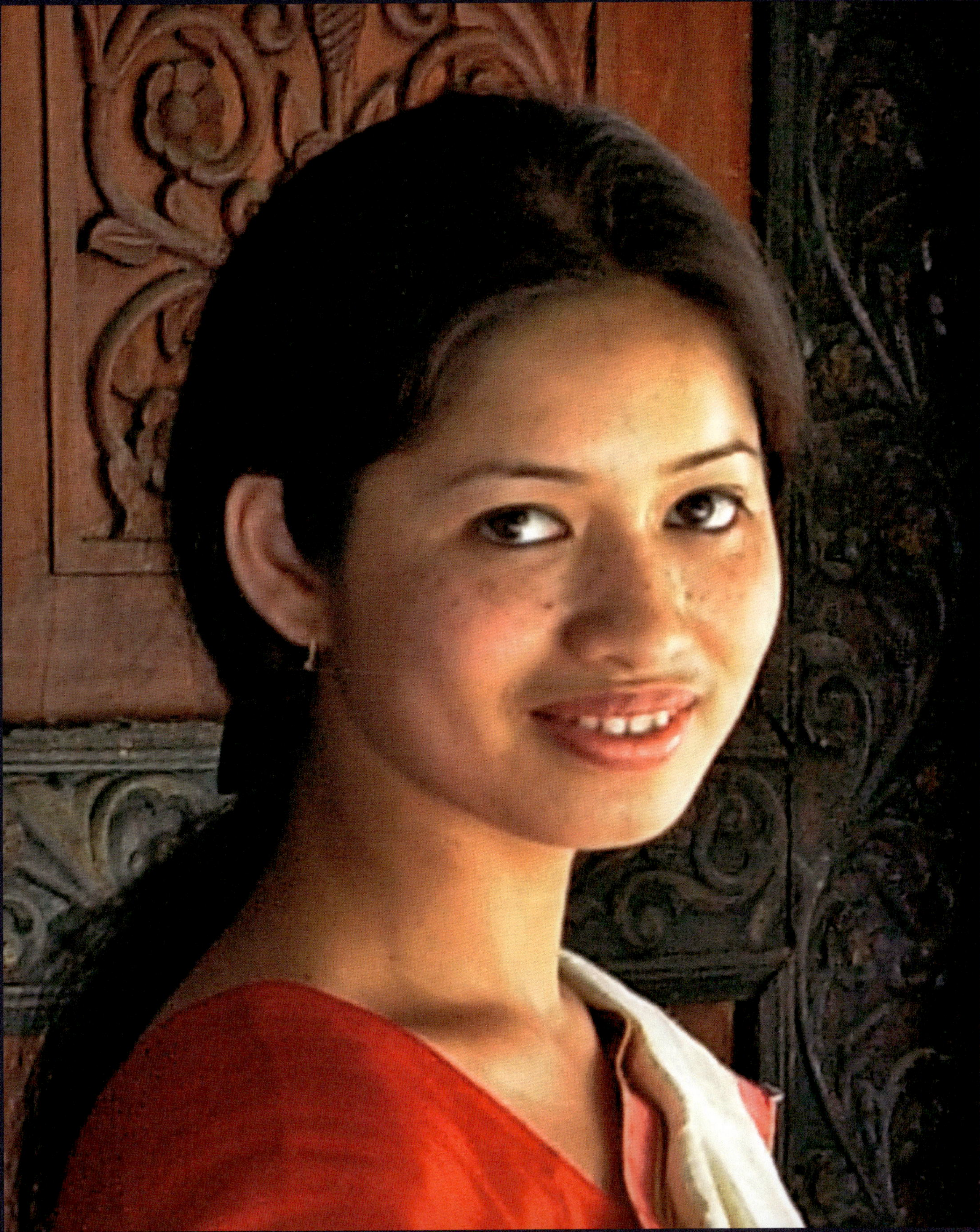

Rabhas, traditionally, do not follow any Brahmanical or Hindu methods of worship. Moreover, the idol worship is totally absent among the Rabhas. They still have practices of ritual sacrifice of certain birds and animals. The ritual sacrifice is an integral part of Rabha religious practices. They consider blood as an essential element to appease their Gods. Usually they sacrifice pigeons and fowls and occasionally pigs for their deities.Like most communities, dances and music play an important part in the lives of the Rabhas. After every ritual they perform various dances. Most of the Rabha women can both sing and dance.

Like most tribal dances, those of the Rabhas are connected to some daily agrarian activity. They have a unique dance form named "Nakchung Reni" to celebrate fishing in the forest brooks. Rabha women of all ages take part in this dance.

Tiwa

Tiwa is a community inhabiting the States of Assam and Meghalaya. They were known as Lalung in the Assamese and Colonial literature and they are still referred so in the Constitution Order of the Government of India .A striking peculiarity of the Tiwa is their division into two sub-groups, Hill Tiwa and Plains Tiwas, displaying very contrasted cultural features.

The Hill Tiwas live in the western most areas of Karbi-Anglong (Assam) as well as in the Northeastern corner of Ri-Bhoi distrcit (Meghalaya). They speak a Tibeto-Burman language of the Bodo-Garo group. They are divided into a dozens of clans recognized by specific names. Their descent system can be said to be Matriarchal.In most cases, the husband goes to live with his wife's family villages and their children are included in their mother's clan. However, in in some cases, today the woman comes to live with his husband and children take his name. This trend is on the rise under the influence of neighbouring populace who are mostly patrilineal. About the half of Hill Tiwas follow their "traditional" religion.

Plains Tiwas live on the plains of the Southern bank of the Brahmaputra valley, mostly in Morigaon and Nagaon districts. The vast majority speaks Assamese as their mother tongue, Tiwa language being still spoken on the

148

foothills and in rare villages of the plains. Their descent system is definitely patrilinear. Their religion practices many elements with Assamese Hinduism, but remains specific.

Rajbongshi

Koch Rajbongshi is an ancient tribe originally from the ancient Koch Kingdom. The Rajbongshi Tribe is referred to as Koch Rajbongshi/Rajbanshi/Rajvanshi. The word Rajbongshi means literally Royal leanage. They have a rich cultural heritage and their own language.
The homelands of this ancient tribe include West Bengal, Assam, Arunachal Pradesh, Meghalaya and various North Eastern parts of India.The language is also spoken in Bangladesh and Nepal. Other names of the language are Kamtapuri, Rajbangsi, Rajbansi, Rajbongshi, Goalpariya and Tajpuri. The Rajbanshi language has a complete grammar. The main dialects are Western Rajbanshi, Central Rajbanshi, Eastern Rajbanshi and Rajbanshi hills also known as koch language.
The Rajbongshi were primarily animists but they have adopted Hindusim

Garo

The Garos are a tribe in Meghalaya, India and neighboring areas of Bangladesh, who call themselves A·chik Mande (literally "hill people," from a·chik "hill" + mande "people") or simply A·chik or Mande..
Their traditional religious system, Songsarek, is generally described as animist. The Garos are mainly distributed over the Kamrup, Goalpara and Karbi Anglong Districts of Assam, Garo Hills in Meghalaya, and substantial numbers, about 200,000 are found in greater Mymensingh (Tangail, Jamalpur, Sherpore, Netrakona) and Gazipur, Rangpur, Sunamgonj, Sylhet, Moulovibazar district of Bangladesh. There are also Garo in the state of Tripura. Garos are also found in minority number in Cooch Behar, Jalpaiguri, Darjeeling and Dinajpur of West Bengal.Garos are also found in minority number in Nagaland but many of the young generations are unable to speak the garo mother tongue.

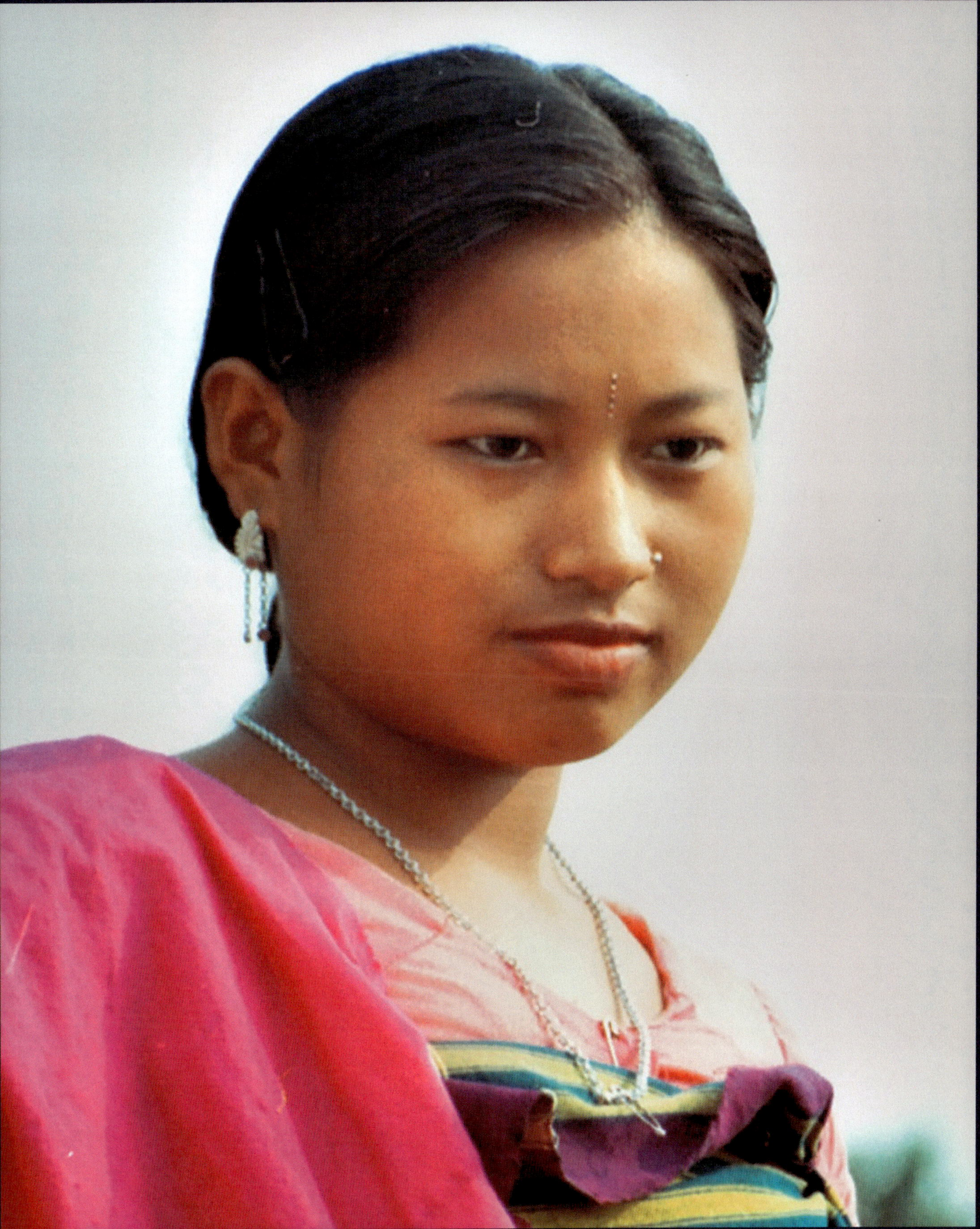

As the Garo language is not traditionally written down, customs, traditions, and beliefs are handed down orally. It is also believed that the written language was lost in its transit to the present Garo Hills.

Garo language has different sub-languages, Viz- A·beng, Atong, Me·gam, Dual,ruga,A'we,chisak, matchi,matabeng,gara,ganching Chibok etc. In Bangladesh A·beng is the usual dialect, but A·chik is used more in India. The Garo language has some similarities with Boro-Kachari, Rava, Dimasa and Kok-Borok languages.

According to one such oral tradition, the Garos first came to Meghalaya from Tibet about 400 (BC)years ago under the leadership of Jappa Jalimpa, crossing the Brahmaputra River and tentatively settling in the river valleyThe earliest written records about the Garo dates from around 1800. They were looked upon as blood thirsty savages, who inhabited a tract of hills covered with almost impenetrable jungle.The Garo had the reputation of being head hunters.

The Garos are one of the few remaining matrilineal societies in the world. The individuals take their clan titles from their mothers. Traditionally, the youngest daughter (nokmechik) inherits the property from her mother. Sons leave the parents' house at puberty, and are trained in the village bachelor dormitory (nokpante). After getting married, the man lives in his wife's house. Garos are only a matrilinear society, but not matriarchal. While property of Garos are owned by the women, the men folk govern it.

Both men and women enjoy adorning themselves with varieties of ornaments. These ornaments are:

    Nadongbi nr sisha – made of a brass ring worn in the lobe of the ear.

    Nadirong – brass ring worn in the upper part of the ear

    Natapsi – string of beads worn in the upper part of the ear

    Jaksan – Bangles of different materials and sizes

    Ripok – Necklaces made of long barrel shaped beads of cornelian or red glass while some are made out of brass or silver and are worn in special occasions.

152

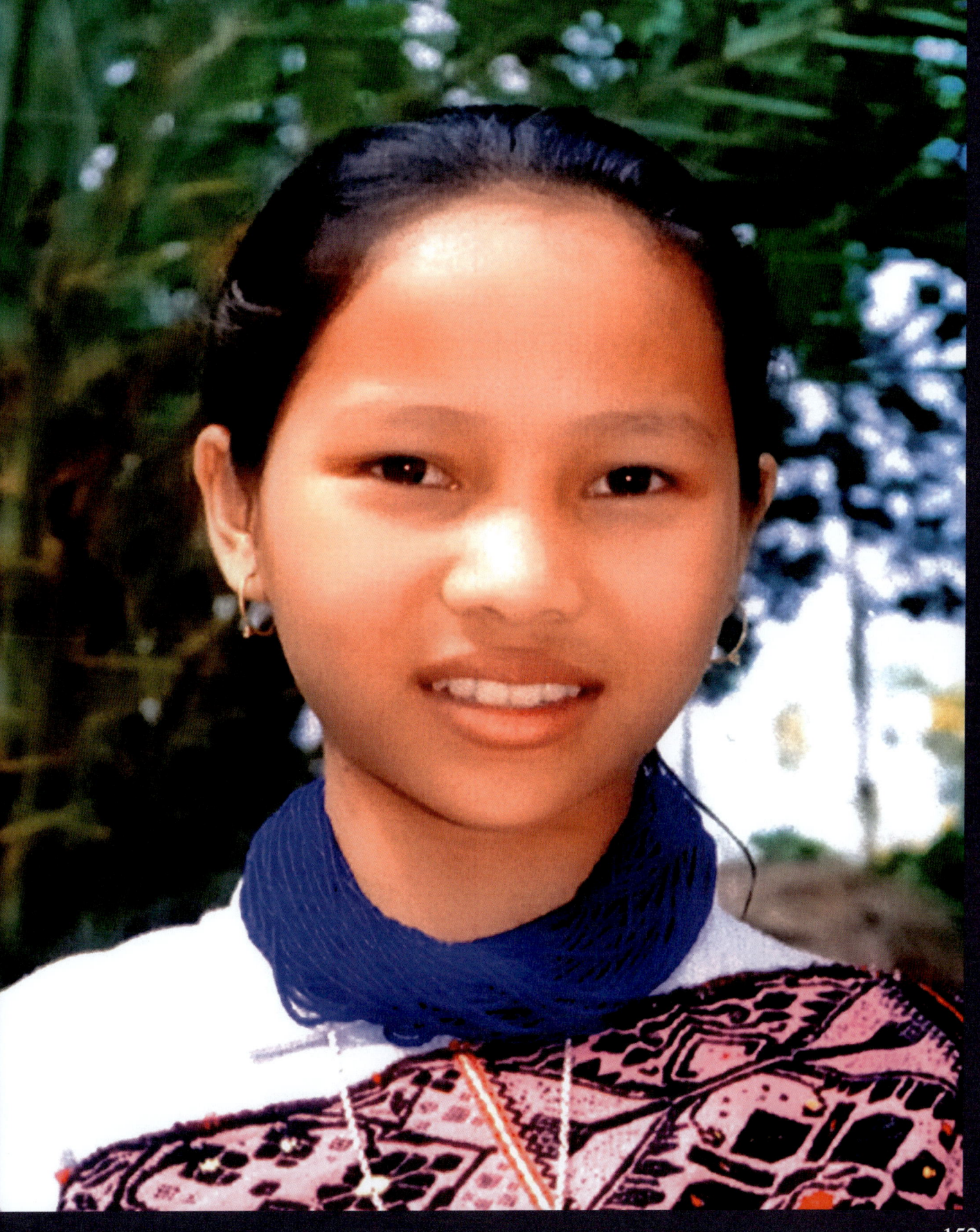

Jaksil – elbow ring worn by rich men on Gana Ceremonies

Penta – small piece of ivory struck into the upper part of the ear projecting upwards parallel to the side of the head

Seng'ki – Waistband consisting of several rows of conch-shells worn by womenPilne – head ornament worn during the dances only by the women

Martially, Garos have their own weapons. One of the principal weapons is two-edged sword called Milam, made of one piece of iron from hilt to point. There is a cross-bar between the hilt and the blade. Other types of weapons are shields, Spear, Bows and Arrows, Axes and Daggers.

The staple food is rice. They also eat millet, maize, tapioca. Garos are very liberal in their food habits. They rear goats, pigs, fowls, ducks and relish dining on them. They also eat other wild animal like deer, bison, wild Boar. Fish, prawns, crabs, eels and dry fish form a part of their diet. Their jhum fields and the forests provide them with a number of vegetables and root for their curry but bamboo shoots are esteemed as a delicacy. They use a kind of potash in curries, which they obtained by burning dry pieces of plantain stems or young bamboos locally known as Kalchi or Katchi. Apart from other drinks country liquor plays an important role in the life of the Garos.

They normally use locally available building materials like timbers, bamboo, cane and thatch. Garo architecture can be classified into following categories:

Nokmong: The house where every A'chik household can stay together. This house is built in such a way that inside the house, there are provisions for sleeping, hearth, sanitary arrangements, kitchen, water storage, place for fermenting wine. A cattle-shed or stall for feeding the cow and the space between the floor and the stilted platform for use as pigsty and in the back of the house, the raised platform serves as hencoop for keeping fowl and for storing firewood, thus every need is fulfilled.

Nokpante: In the Garo habitation, the house where unmarried male youth or bachelors live is called Nokpante. The word Nokpante is a bachelor's hostel. Nokpantes are generally constructed in the front

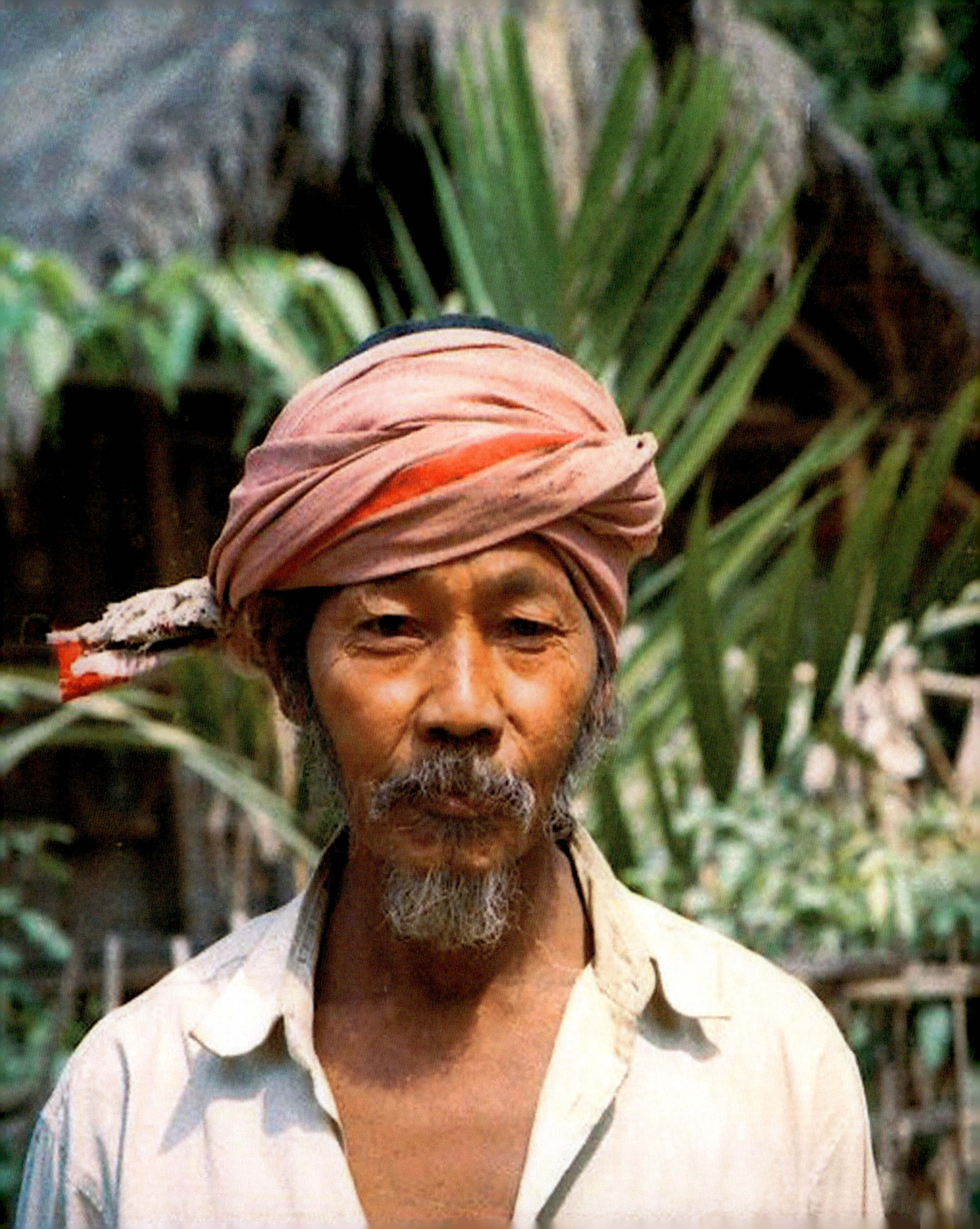

courtyard of the Nokma, the chief's house . The art of cultivation, various arts and cultures forms, and different games are taught in the Nokpante to the young boys by elders.

Jamsreng: In certain areas, in the rice field or orchards, small huts are constructed. They are called Jamsireng or Jamdap. Either the season's fruits or grains are collected and stored in the Jamsreng or it can be used for sleeping and keeping watch of the matured fruits.

Jamatdal: The small house, a type of miniature house, built in the jhum fields is called Jamatdal or 'field house'. In certain places, where there is danger from wild animals, a small house with ladder is constructed on the treetop. This is called Borang or 'house on the treetop'.

The common and regular festivals are those connected with agricultural operations.

Greatest among Garo festivals is the Wangala, usually celebrated in October or November, is thanks-giving after harvesting in which Saljong, the patron God of bountiful harvest and safe keeping of the village is appeased. Other festivals are Gal·mak Doa and Agalmaka among others.

There used to be a celebration of 100 drum festival in Asanang near Tura in West Garo Hills, Meghalaya, usually in the month of October or November. Thousands of people especially the young people gather at Asanang and celebrate Wangala with great joy. Beautiful Garo girls known as nomil and handsome young men pante take part in 'Wangala' festivals. The 'pante's beat is a kind of long drum called dama in groups accompanied by bamboo flute. The 'nomil's with colorful costume dance to the tune of dama' 'and sing folk songs in a circle. Most of the folk songs depict ordinary garo life, God's blessings,the beauty of nature, day to day struggles, romance and human aspirations.

The annual winter festival AHAIA . The three-day fest feature a gala event with cultural show, food festival, rock concert, wine drinking, angling competition, ethnic wear competition, and modern carnival games.

assam,the Golden Valley

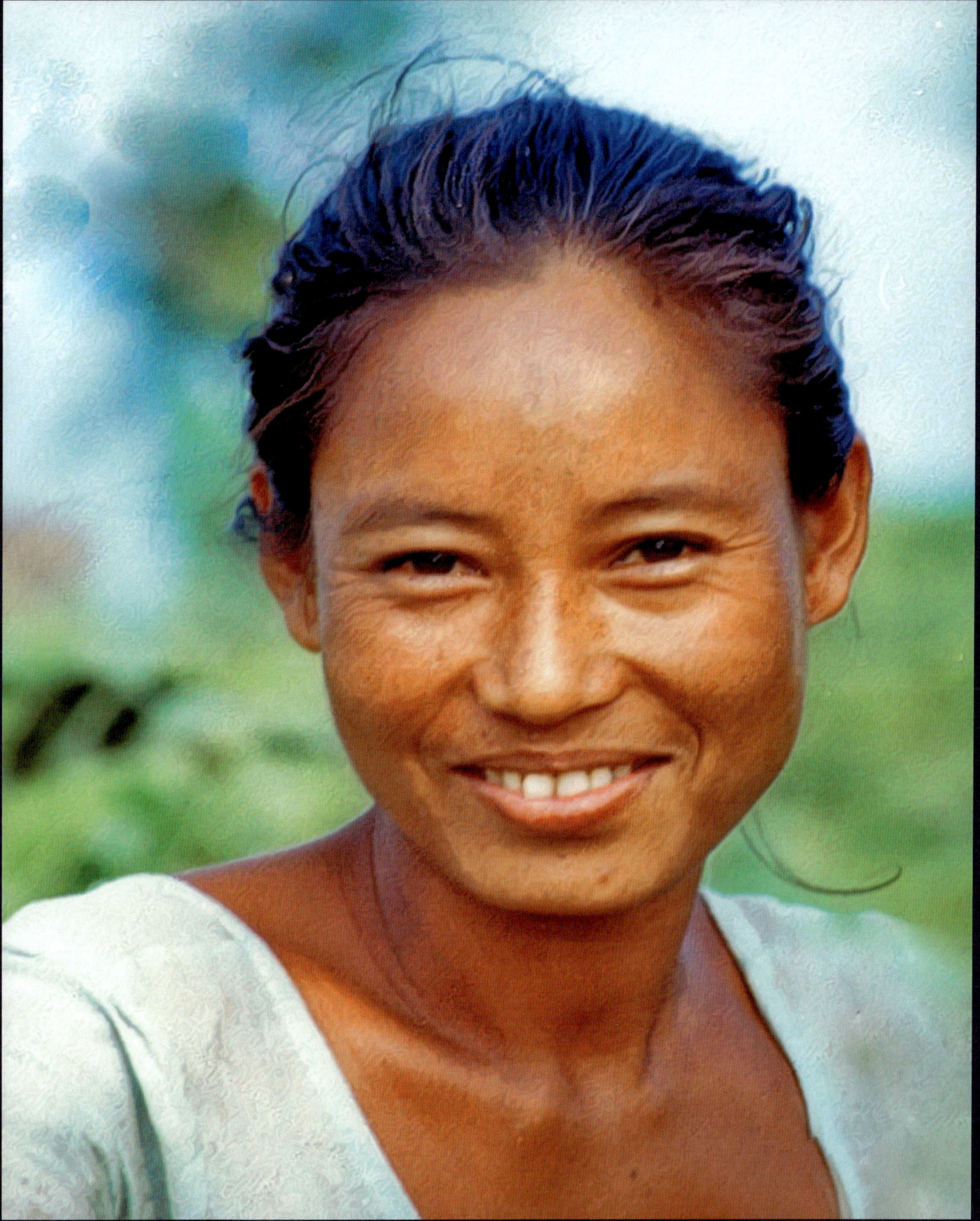

Group songs may include Nangorere, Serejing, Pandu Dolong. Dance forms are Ajema Roa, Mi Sua, Chambil Moa, Dokru Sua, Kambe Toa, Gaewang Roa, Napsepgrika and many others.

The traditional Garo musical instruments are:

Idiophones: Self-sounding and made of resonant materials – Kakwa, Nanggilsi, Guridomik, Kamaljakmora, all kinds of gongs, Rangkilding, Rangbong, Nogri etc.

Aerophone: Wind instruments –Adil, Singga, Sanai, Kal, Bolbijak, Illep or Illip, Olongna, Tarabeng, Imbanggi, Akok or Dakok, Bangsi rosi, Tilara or Taragaku, Bangsi mande, Otekra, Wa·pepe or Wa·pek.

Chordophone: Stringed instruments – Dotrong, Sarenda, Chigring, Dimchrang or Kimjim, Gongmima or Gonggina.

Membranophone: Which have skins or membranes stretched over a frame – Ambeng Dama, Chisak Dama, Atong Dama, Garaganching Dama, Ruga and Chibok Dama, Dual-Matchi Dama, Nagra, Kram .

Bodo

The Bodos(Boros) represents one of the largest of the 18 ethnic sub-groups within the Bodo-Kacharis group. Bodos have settled in most areas of North-East India, and parts of Nepal. Among the 18 groups mentioned, the Mech live in Western Assam, the Bodo in central Assam, the Dimasa and Hojai to the north of Cachar Hills, and the Sonowal and Thengal in the eastern part of the Brahmaputra are all closely related.
They represent one of the largest ethnic and linguistic groups of the valley. Typical Bodo last names surnames are Bargayary, Basumatary, Bodosa, Boro, Brahma, Bwiswmuthiary, Dwimary, Goyary, Hazowary, Ishlary, Ishwary, Khaklary, Mushahary, Narzary, Narzihary,Narzinary, Owary, Sargwary, Sibigry and Wary.

assam,the Golden Valley

158

The traditional favorite drink of the Bodos is Zu Mai (Zu:wine, Mai:rice). Rice is the staple diet of the Bodos and is often accompanied by a non vegetarian dish such as fish or pork. Traditionally Bodos are non-vegetarians.

Weaving is another integral part of Bodo culture. Many families rear their own silkworms, the cocoons of which are then spun into silk. Bodo girls learn to weave from a young age, and no Bodo courtyard is complete without a loom. Most women weave their own Dokhnas (the traditional dress of the Bodo women) and shawls. The Bodos are also expert bamboo craftsmen.

In the past, Bodos worshipped their forefathers. In recent years, Bodos practice Bathouism, Hinduism.

Bathouism is a form worshipping forefathers called Obonglaoree. The siju plant is(taken as the symbol of Bathou and) worshipped.

In the Bodo Language Ba means five and thou means deep. Five is a significant number in the Bathou religion.

A clean surface near home or courtyard could be an ideal for worship. Usually, one pair of Betelnut called 'goi' and betel leaf called 'pathwi' could be used as offering. On some occasion, worship offering could include rice, milk, and sugar. For the Kherai Puja, the most important festival of the Bodos, the altar is placed in the rice field. Other important festivals of the Bodos include Hapsa Hatarnai, Awnkham Gwrlwi Janai, Bwisagu and Domashi.

assam,the Golden Valley

160

There are smaller groups of people speaking Phake, Aiton, Khamti, Khamyang some of the Tai languages. The Tai-Ahom language (brought by Sukaphaa and his followers), which is no more a spoken language today but is prevalent due to centuries long care and preservation by the Bailungs (traditional priests).

Tai Phake

The Tai-Phake people were believed to have migrated from the Shan kindom Mong Mao (Muang Mao), Myanmar in the 18th century. The word Phake has been derived from the Tai words 'Pha' meaning wall and 'Ke' meaning ancient or old.

Prior to their immigration into Assam, they were residents on the banks of the Nam Turung or Turung Pani. They first settled under their chief Chow Ta Meng Khuen Meng of the royal line of Mung Kong at a place called Moongkongtat. On their arrival in Assam, they settled in the rich south bank of the Buridihing River, which came to be known as Namphake.

Significant population of Tai-Phake people are found in Dibrugarh, Tinsukia districts of Assam and Lohit and Changlang districts of Arunachal Pradesh. The village with most population of the Tai-Phake people is in Namphake village. Besides Namphake, they are also found in Tipamphake, Borphake, Manmau, Namchai, Manlong, Nanglai, Ninggum, Phaneng, Lalung (Bordumsa) villages.

The Tai-Phakes are essentially democratic and simple. Although the people do not possess any formal council, yet the meeting of the village elders headed by the "gaonbura" exercises the highest legal and judicial powers. Any dispute among the people are settled by the village monks known as "chou-mouns". The Tai-Phakes possess a written code called "thamchat", which is referred to by the village elders while deciding of local nature. The penalties for breaches of law, the idea of right and wrong, appear to be genuinely indigenous to their culture. The rules of conduct that the "thamchat" enjoins on its members are mainly based on ethical principles.

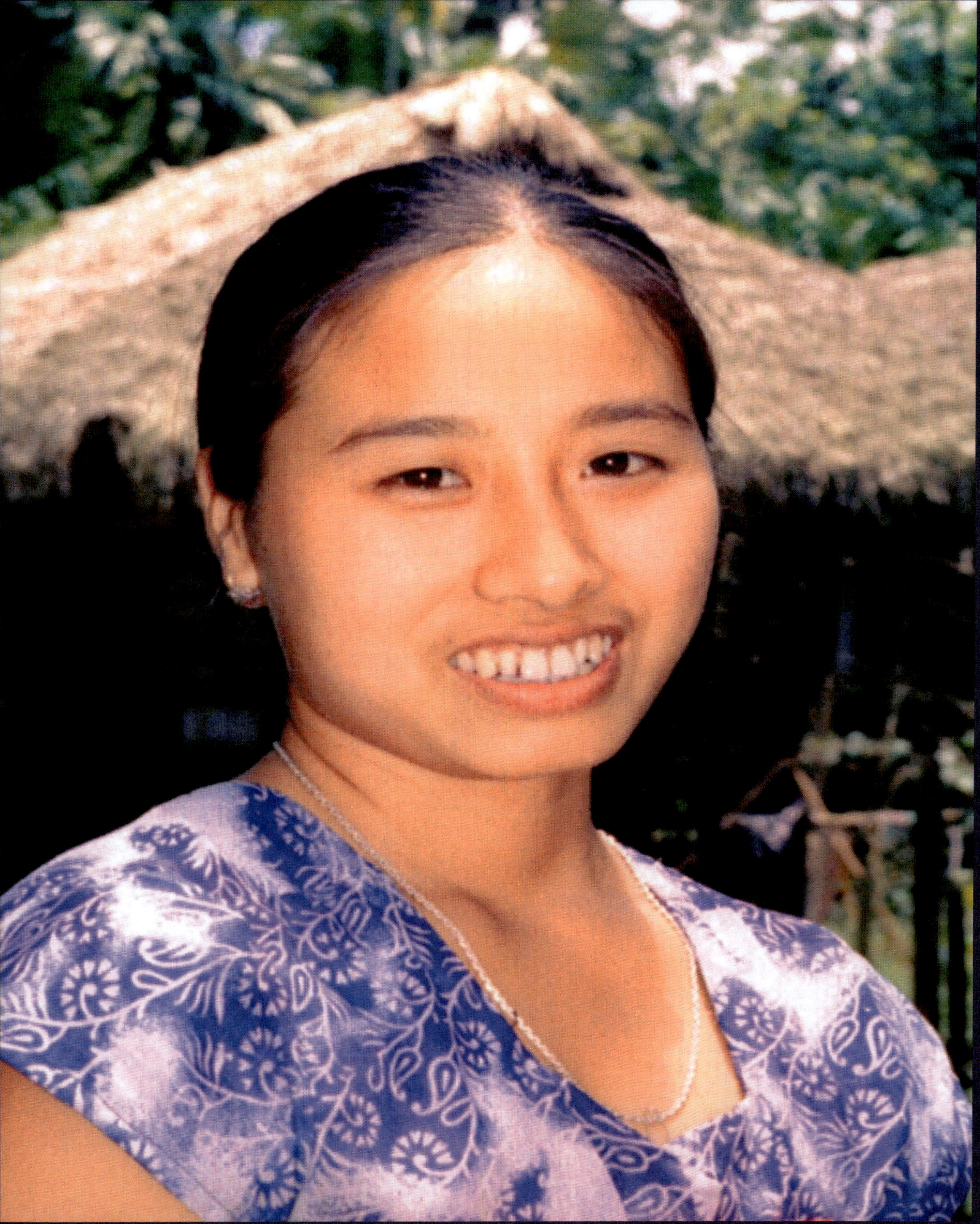

The Tai-Phakes usually marry within the community. The society is basically patriarchal . They are monogamous although polygamy is not forbidden provided the man has the requisite means to support such a family. The Tai-Phakes do not keep any matrimonial relations with people of other caste or tribes. Widow and cross cousin marriage take place in the Tai-Phake society. The marriage is performed with a elaborate ceremony

The Tai-Phakes believe in the existence of sprit and certain rituals are observed to appease to malevolent sprits. Sympathetic magic is practiced and efficacy of mantras is believed by them. Normsl personal ailmentsare addressed by the Tai-Phakes with their indigenous supernatural methods.

The Tai-Phake people are bilingual. They speak Phake language among themselves and speak Assamese with an outsider. The Phake language is similar to those of Shan. They have their own separate scripts and also have preserved their manuscripts in their religious scriptures.Being followers of Theravada Buddhism, some of the Tai-Phake people are also able to read Pali.

The houses of the Tai-Phakes are chang-ghars.,built on piles of wood known as "haun hang". Materials is like takau (toko paat) leaves, timber and bamboos are used in the construction of their houses. There are two hearths in each house and the inside one is considered sacred. Every house has a drawing room called "kan nok", a prayer room called "khok tang-som" with a kitchen called "haun aom".

The Tai-Phake women wear colourful dresses woven by them. Their outfit consists of an ankle-long skirt ("chin"), a blouse open at the front ("nang-wat") and fastened around the armpits and a girdle ("chai-chin") to tighten the skirt around the waist. The female child wears a skirt ("chin") and a blouse. A white turban ("phahu") is worn by the women folk on individual preference. The colours of their dresses are expressive of their ages. The girls wear white sarongs; women stripped red, yellow and green sarongs and old women deep purple and blue sarongs with stripes. The men wear lungis known as "phanoot", a kurta, and a folded chadar.

assam,the Golden Valley

164

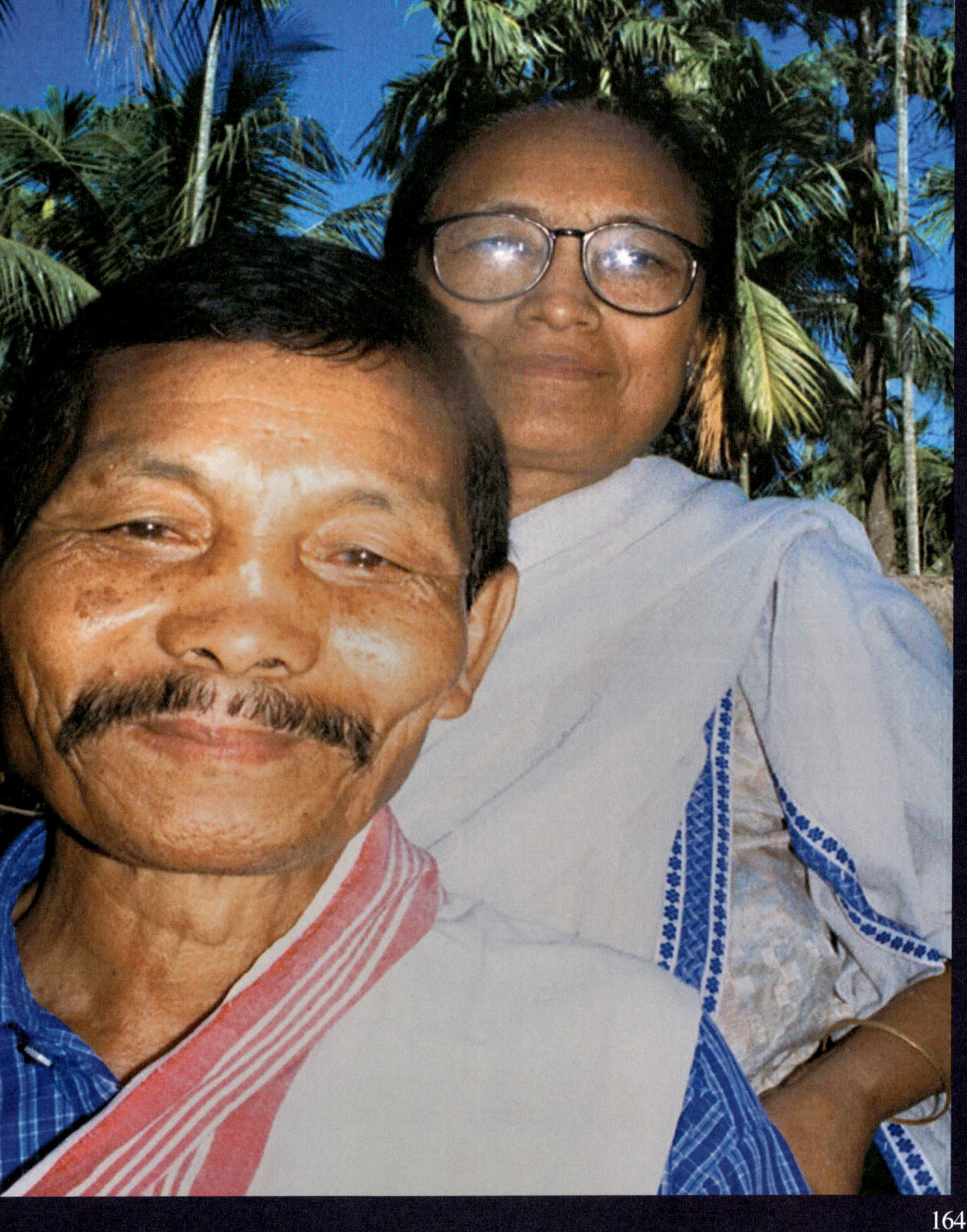

Poi Sangken is the major festival of the Tai-Phakes. It is similar to Songkran which is celebrated in Thailand. It marks the beginning of new year in the Tai calendar. It is celebrated for three days. Basically it starts from 13th or 14th of April every year. In this festival people throw water on each other which signifies washing away the sins of one another. They also cleanse Buddha images and statues from household shrines as well as from monasteries by gently pouring water over them.

Buddha Purnima is also a major festival of the Tai-Phakes. It marks the birthday of Lord Gautama Buddha. On this day the people gather together in the Buddhist Monastery and offer prayers to the God. This is followed by a feast. Generally this festival falls in the month of May.
Naun-wa is a three-month period in which no marriages or construction work are done. This period is considered to be inauspicious. In each month during the day of "purnima" the people of the village gather together in the monastery and offer prayers. It is not festival but an important religious practice.Poi Ok-wa is celebrated after the three-months period of "Naun-wa". It marks the end of "Naun-wa". People from different villages and a union of monks gather together offer prayers to God to forgive them for their shortcomings
Poi Mai-ko-chum-fai is a festival which is celebrated during the full moon day of February month. Small piles of wood and hay are set on fire by the people at late evening of this day. During this occasion they prepare traditional dishes like "khau-laam".In addition to above the Tai-Phake people also celebrate festivals like Poi Lu-fra, Poi Lu-kyong, Poi Kithing.
Rice is the staple food of the Tai-Phakes. Their meals consist of cooked or steamed rice wrapped in banana or tara or kau leaves that known as "khau how" and boiled vegetables. Moreover a large number of wild leafy vegetables such as "pukut", "khi kai" are eaten by them.Their meals comprise of meat, fish, eggs, steamed rice, dry fish, sour fish, dry meat, rice cakes. Tea is their favorite beverage. Killing of animals is prohibited so hunting is not practiced by the Tai-Phakes.
Cremation is the rule . The purificatory ceremony, in case of normal death is observed on the seventh day after death. Entertainment of the villagers with a feast and gift to the monks are the salient features of their purification ceremony.

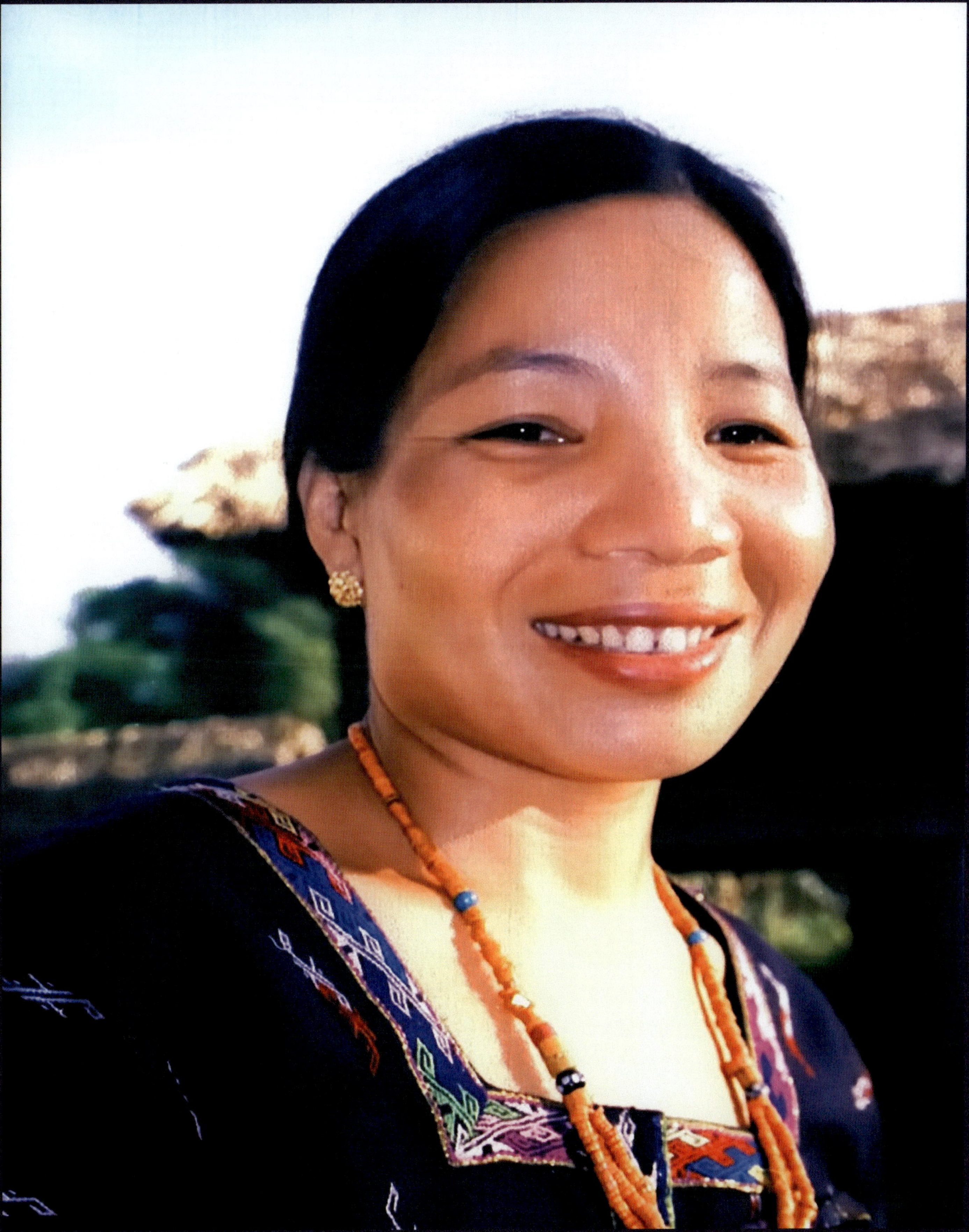

The Tai-Phakes have special provision for the disposal of the dead body of a monk. The monk's dead body is not disposed on the same day, rather it is kept for a year or so in a watertight coffin. After about one year a big festival is arranged and all the Tai-Phakes of different villages are invited and the dead body of the monk is ceremonially cremated.

The major occupation of the Tai-Phake people is agriculture. They cultivate crops like rice paddy, mustard, potatoes. Besides agriculture they also have other subsidiary sources of income from which the people earn good income. They also rear cattle, buffaloes. Fishing is a major practice of the Tai-Phakes.

Singpho

The Singpho people of Arunachal Pradesh inhabit the district of Lohit and Changlang and the Kachin State of Burma. Some are also found in the Tinsukia district of Assam. Comprising a population size of 7,200 in India, they live in 12 villages, namely Dibang, Ketetong, Pangna, Ulup, Ingthem, Mungbhon, Pangsun, Hasak, Katha, Bisa, Namo and Kumsai. They are the same people as those called the Kachin in Burma and the Jingpo in China. They speak the Singpho dialect of the Jingpo language.

The Singphos are divided into a number of clans, each under a Chief known as Gam. The principal Gams include the Bessa, Duffa, Luttao, Luttora, Tesari, Mirip, Lophae, Lutong and Magrong. The Singpho are also divided into four classes, namely Shangai, Myung, Lubrung and Mirip.

Like the Khampti, the are Theravada Buddhist by religion. In memorial of Gautama Buddha, the Songken festival is celebrated in April. Spiritual worship (nat) is also practised as well in addition to Buddhism. According to their belief, malevolent and responsible spirits causing miseries to mankind were worshipped on ceremonies and spirits like Ningsenat, Multung-Dingna, Cit-Hungnat, Natkum, Mainat, are given offerings of sacrifice of cattle such as bulls, cows as also pigs, fowl to appease the spirits. They also believed that God uses rainbow as the ladder to meet his wife on the moon.

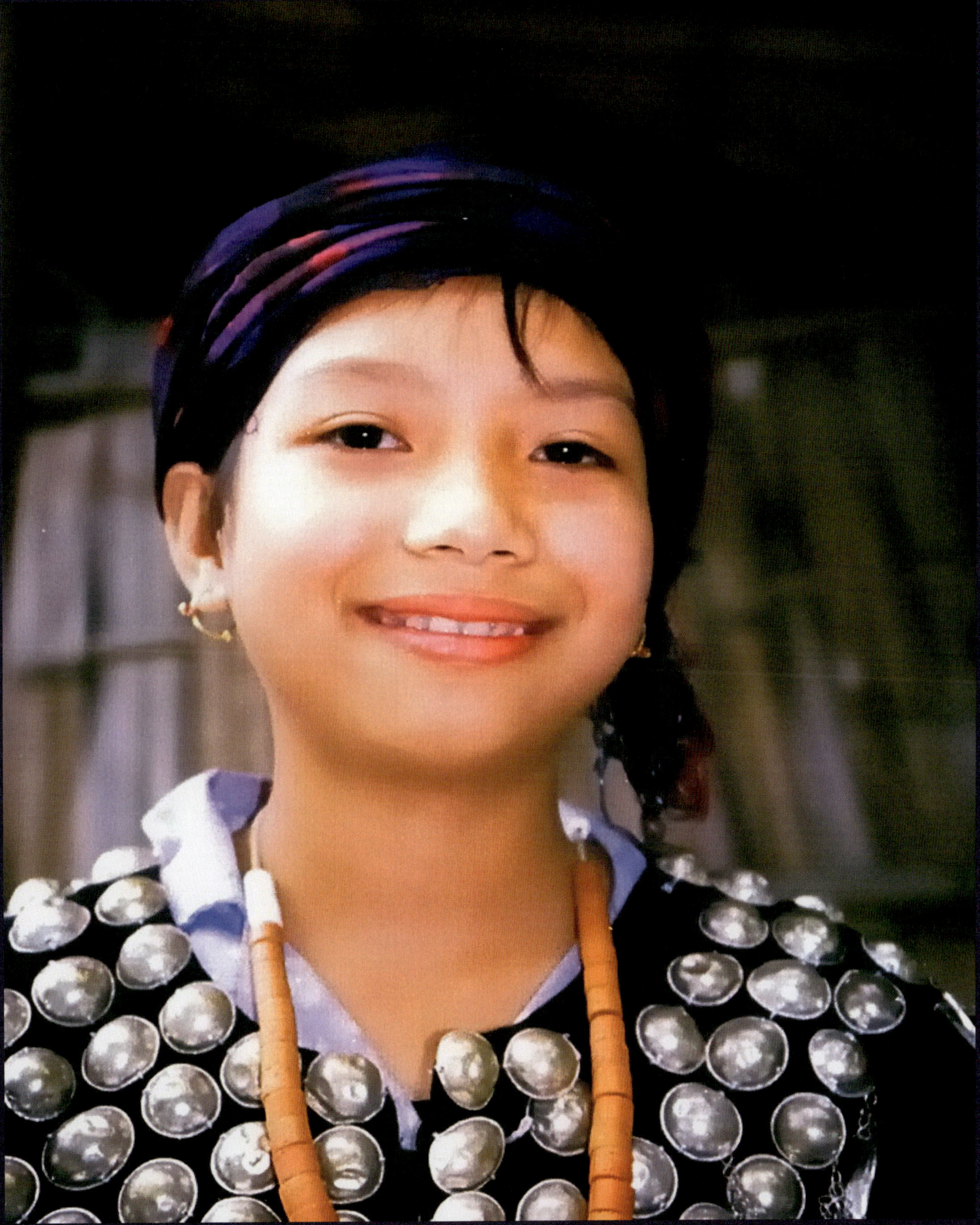

Unlike most hill-people, shifting cultivation (Jhum) is not as widely practiced, although tea is widely planted. The Singpho produce their tea by plucking the tender leaves and drying them in the sun and exposing to the night dew for three days and nights. The leaves are then placed in the hollow tube of a bamboo, and the cylinder will be exposed to the smoke of the fire. In this way, their tea can be kept for years without losing its flavor. The Singpho also depended on yams and other edible tubers as a staple substitute.

Most men tie their hair in a large knot on the crown of the head. The women dress their hair gathered into a broad knot on the crown of the head, fastening it by silver bodkins, chains and tassels, which is similar to the architecture of the modern skyscraper. The maidens tie their tresses into a roll and keep it tied just above the nape.

The Singpho uses the Burmese pasto as an undergarment, which is woven from colored cloth or silk in check pattern. A colored cotton jacket is worn over the upper portion. Many chiefs adopted the Shan or Burmese costumes. The Singpho women wear a cloth similar to the Assamese mekhela that is tied at the breast, which reaches to little below the knee. The men occasionally wear small earrings, although the women wear large pieces of amber ear studs on their ears. The men lightly tattooed their limbs, arm and shoulders. At the same time, the married women also tattooed their legs from the ankle to the knee in broad parallel bands which consist of eight bars in alternate black and white. However, the unmarried women are not permitted to tattoo at all.

Khamti

The Khamti, whose name is also spelled as Hkamti by the Burmese and Khampti by the Assamese, is a sub-group of the Shan people found in the Sagaing Division, Hkamti District in northwestern Burma as well as Lohit district of Arunachal Pradesh in India. Smaller numbers can be found in parts of Assam as well as the East Siang district of Arunachal Pradesh
The Khamti who inhabit the region around the Tengapani basin were descendants of migrants who came during the 18th century from the Bor-Khampti region, the mountainous valley of the Irrawaddy. The Khamti possess East Asian features.

170

The Khamti are followers of Theravada Buddhism, though many are non-vegetarians. The Khamti adopted a script of Shan origin, known as Lik-Tai for their language.

The Khamti society is divided into classes, each signifying distinct status in the social hierarchy. The chiefs occupy the highest positions, followed by the priests, who wield considerable influence over all ranks. In the past, the slaves constituted the lowest rank.

Houses of the Khamti are built on raised stilts with thatched roofs. The roofs are constructed so low that the walls remain concealed. Wooden planks are used for flooring and the walls are made of bamboo splices. There are separate dormitories for the unmarried ladies and bachelors. Dormitories play an important role in the Khamti society.

Each village has its dormitory, with young girls at one end and young boys at the other. A girl who becomes an inmate of the Girls' dormitory never sleeps at home, although she always returns home for meals. The Virgins' house is considered to be a sacred place and is in the charge of older maidens. The Khamti are settled agriculturists. Unlike other tribes, they use the plough (Thai) drawn by a single animal, either an oxen or a buffalo.

The Khamti raise crops such as paddy rice (khapu), mustard (hanio) and potato (man kala). Their staple food is rice, usually supplemented by vegetables, meat and fish. They also drink a beer made from rice (thou) as a beverage.

The traditional Khamti dress of men consisted of a blue, tight-fitting jacket of cotton cloth. They also wear a full sleeved cotton shirt (siu pajai) and the deep-coloured lungi (phanoi). The women's dresses consists of a half-sleeved blouse (siu pajao), a deep-coloured skirt (siu) made from cotton or silk, and a coloured silk scarf.[3] Their jewelry consists of bright amber earrings and coral and bead necklaces. The Khamti men usually tattoo their bodies upon visiting their relatives in Burma.

The Khamti tie their hair into a large knot, which is supported by a white turban. The chiefs wear a Chinese coat made of silk.

assam, the Golden Valley

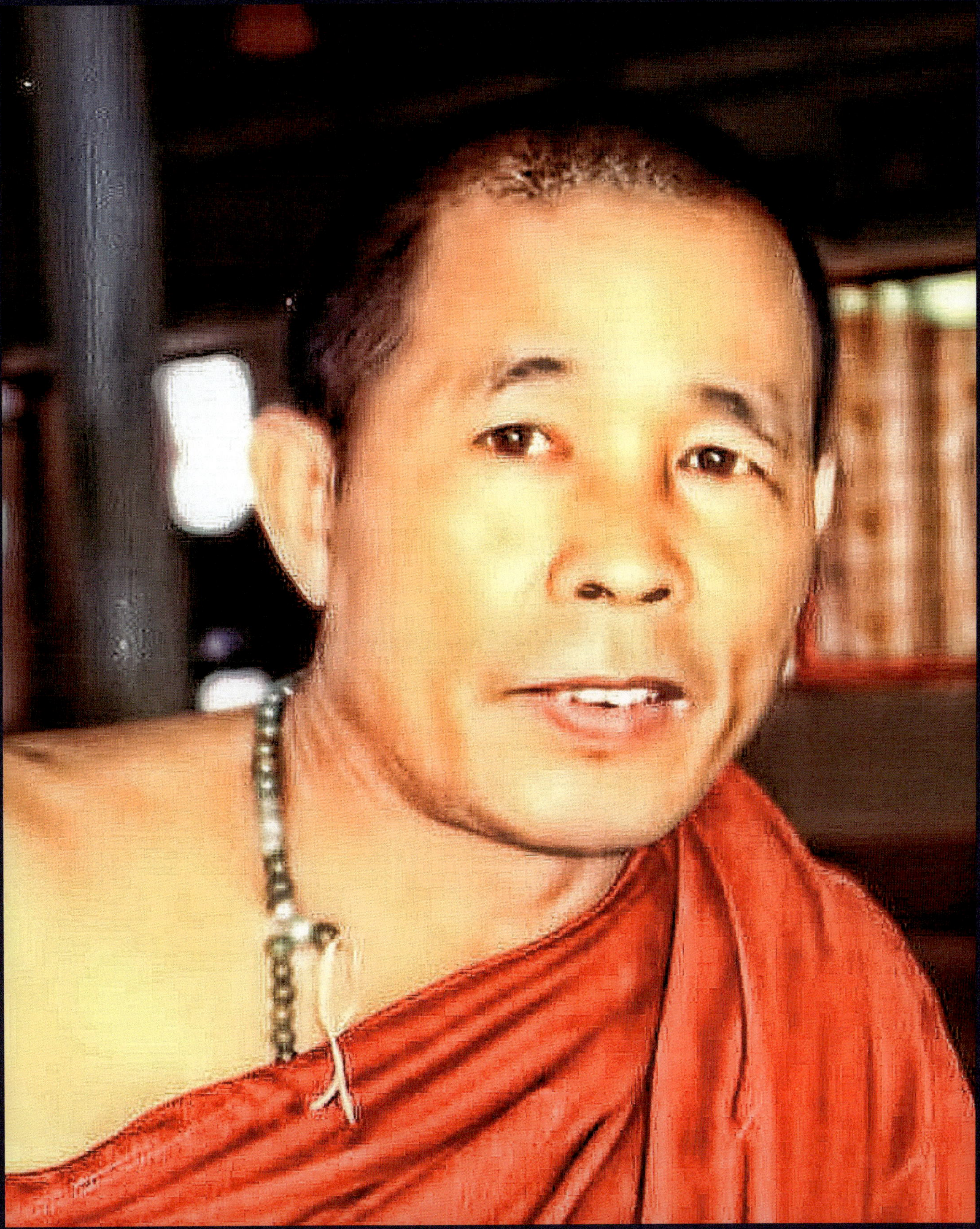

The Khamti women tie their hair in the "sky-scraper" style. The hair is drawn up from the back and sides in one massive roll, measuring four to five inches in length. An embroidered band, with the fringed and tasseled ends hangs down behind, encircles the roll.

The Khamti are renowned for their craftsmanship. Their sword (known as dao) is well-known by people from Assam. Their priests are also known to be amateur craftsmen, who use wood, bone or ivory to carve out religious statues.

It is believed that by shaping ivory handles of weapons they will evince great skill. Their weapons include poisoned bamboo spikes (panjis), spear, bow and arrow, sword, and shield, usually made of rhinoceros or buffalo hide. The Khamti also have firearms which resemble old flint muskets and horse pistols. The sword is carried on the frontal part of the body, so that its hilt can be grasped in the right hand if needed.

Aiton

The Aiton ethnic group inhabits villagesin the Jorhat and Karbi-Along districts ofAssam State in north-east India. The ancestors of the Aiton originated in northern Myanmar, where they lived for centuries along with other Tai-speakinggroups. 'In the latter part of the eighteenth century, the Aiton entered Assam as political refugees
from the Shan State in Burma. They speak the Aiton language among themselves and Assamese, Hindi and English with others.

Aiton is believed to be similar to the Shan language spoken in Myanmar, China and Thailand, but after more than two centuries of separation from their homeland, the Aiton language, culture and identity have gradually been assimilated.

Elders among the Aiton are responsible for handing the oral traditions, folk tales and songs about their origin and migration down to the next generation. Their songs tell of oppression in their original homeland, which led to their long and diffi cult journey across the mountains into India.Until the past decade all Aiton were farmers, fishermen and hunters, but in recent years an increasing number of people have become businessmen, teachers and laborers in the nearby townships in both the government and private sectors. Despite their small population, there are,14 different clans among the Aiton. These days the people use their respective clan names as their surnames.

174

The strict marriage customs of the Aiton mean that a young man must marry his maternal uncle's daughter. A bride price is required, whereby the family of the groom must pay an agreed-upon amount of cash and goods to the family of the bride. In part this is an expression of gratitude to the bride's family for their years of expense in raising her. Buddhist monks are called upon to officiate the wedding ceremony, which is held at the bride's house. After giving birth an Aiton woman must not interact with other members of the community for a full month, as she is considered 'polluted'. After the month has passed a ritual is performed and the new mother is free to return to society. All Aiton are followers of Theravada Buddhism, which they brought with them when they migrated into India more than 200 years ago. They also 'worship Medham-Medhphi, their deity, every morning and evening.

Turung

Turung (Tibeto-Burman) is spoken by around 1,200 people in six villages in Assam, India. Turung historical chronicles indicate that the Turungs are descended from Tai speaking people who lived for a time among the Singphos, whose Tibeto-Burman language, closely related to Jinghpaw spoken in Burma, they then acquired. Since around 1800 they have lived near to and intermarried with Tai speaking Aitons. Today their language is mostly Singpho mixed with Tai.Turung speakers in Balipathar display a high level of Assamese mixed in their speech.

Assamese or Tai. There are reasons to use each of the scripts. The related Jinghpaw language of Burma uses Roman script, and many people regard the Roman script as 'more modern' and thus more suitable. On the other hand Assamese script is understood by all and those Turungs who have written down songs or stories have usually done so using Assamese script. Tai script is favoured by those who associate themselves most strongly with their Tai heritage.

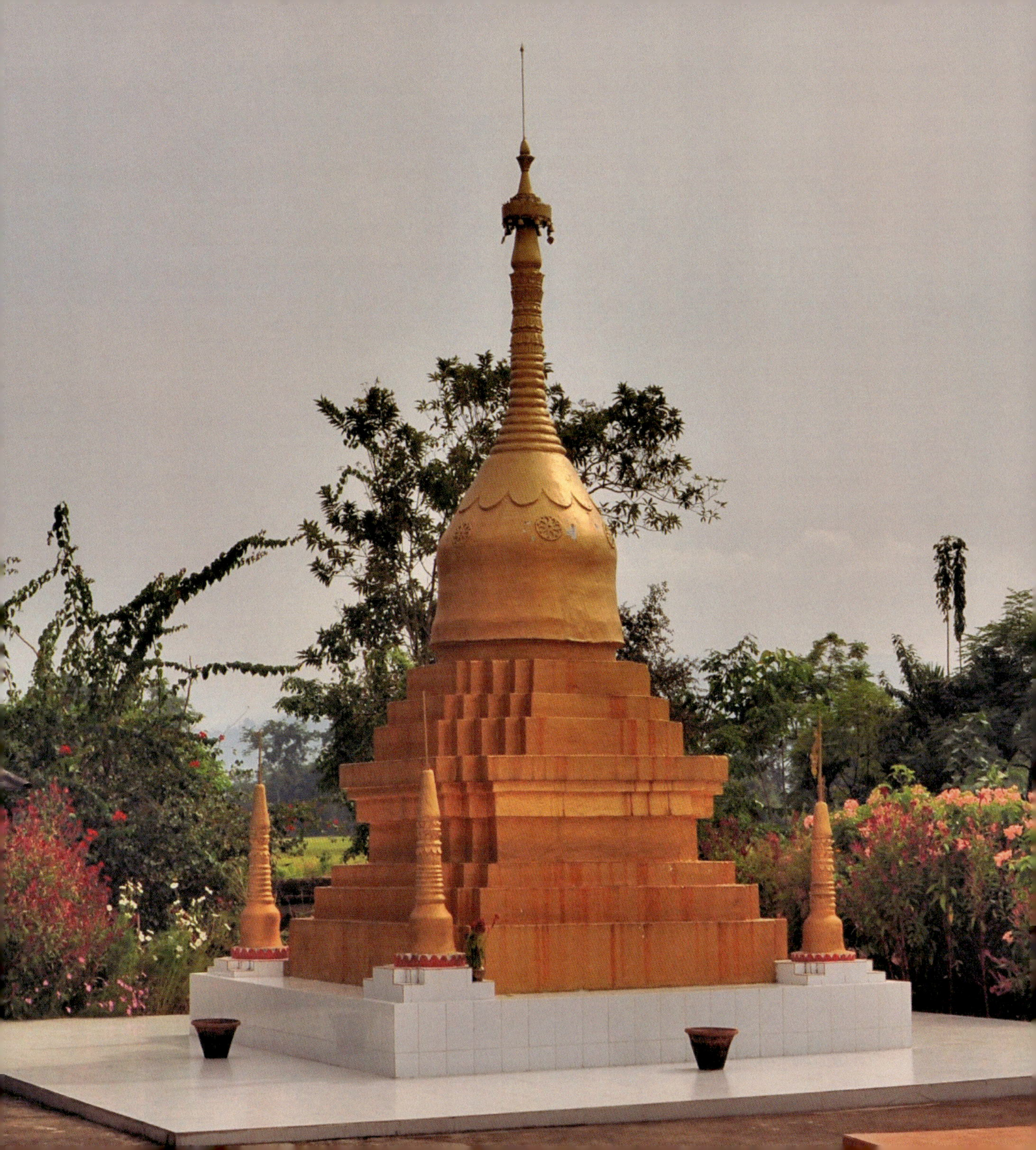

Ancient Assam

350
Pushya Varman establishes the Varman dynasty in Kamarupa

636
Xuanzang visits the court of Bhaskarvarman in Kamarupa.

650
Bhaskarvarman dies. End of Varman dynasty

655
Salasthamba establishes Mlechchha dynasty in Kamarupa

900
Brahmapala establishes Pala dynasty in Kamarupa

1100
Jayapala, the last Pala king removed by Ramapala of Gaur

Medieval Assam

1185
Prithu establishes the Khen dynasty and the Kamata kingdom

1187
Birpal establishes Chutiya kingdom

Brief History

It is one of the few places in the world where people from Indo-Aryan, Austro-Asiatic and Tibeto –Burman and Mon-Khamer have found a reason to live together and form a common society –Assamese. Historically the region is mentioned and has archeological sites covering the;
Paleolithic remains in the Garo Hills, Arunachal Pradesh and Manipur, dating back to the period 781,000 to 126,000 years ago.
Neolithic cultures sites in Kamrup and North Cachar Hills.
Megalithic remains in Khasi & Jayantia Hills and Nagaland.
Myth logically, it is mentioned in the *Kalika Purana*, *Mahabharata* and the *Yogini Tantra*

Assam's prehistoric origins are constructed with references of the land in the Epics. The first non Aryan King was Mahiranga of the *Danava Dynasty* which was subsequently conquered by Narakasura, a scion of the *Naraka Dyynasty*. As per legend the last of the Naraka kings was slain by *Lord Krishna* and thereafter his son Bhagadatta took over the throne. Bhagadatta is mentioned to have fought in the war of *Mahabharata* with a army of Easterners. His kingdom was called *Pragjotishpur*.

Rukmininati or the ruins of Princess Rukmini kingdom is situated at the heart of Chimiri village which is approximately 12 km from Roing. You find the remains of burnt and baked bricks, pottery, which indicates the progress of the erstwhile civilization in the 4th. Century. There is also a hill-fort presumably of 14th/15th century.

Historically, the earliest kingdom was established by *Pushya Varman* of the Varman Dynasty at Kamrupa in the 4th Century. Although, an aboriginal kingdom, it drew its origins from the *Naraka* Dynasty. **Bhaskarvarman** in the 7th century was the most influential king of the dynasty. He died heirless and the reins passed on to *Salasthamba* who started the **Melchchha** dynasty, who ruled for almost 200 years.

13th century

1228
Sukaphaa enters Assam

1253
Sukaphaa establishes capital at Charaideo

15th century

1449
Srimanta Sankardev is born

1490
First Ahom-Kachari battle

1498
Hussein Shah of Gaur removes the last Khen ruler of Kamata kingdom
Vasco da Gama lands at Calicut

16th century

1515
Vishwa Singha establishes Koch dynasty

1522
Chutiya kingdom annexed to Ahom Kingdom under Suhungmung

1527
The first Muslim invasion of the Ahom kingdom ends in failure.

1532
Turbak attacks Ahom Kingdom, the first commander to enjoy some success.

At the end of this dynastic rule a new leader was chosen in **Brahmapala**,who intiated the Pala dynasty. The last Pala king was removed by a Gaur king **Ramapala** in 1110 . Although the two subsequent kings **Timgyadeva** and **Vidyadeva** ruled independently they operated under the tutelage of the Kamrupa Kingdom.In the 12th century the Kamrupa Kingdom finally fragmented into independent Kingdoms.

The medieval period saw the development of then **Kamata** Kingdom to the west of the earstwhile Kamrupa Kingdom which finally divided into **Koch Bihar** and **Koch Hajo** Kingdoms.

In the East there developed the **Chutia** and the **Kachari**Kingdoms and in between the Bhuyan Chiefs established their own **Bhuyan** Kingdom.

It was during this period, precisely 1228, **Sukhapa** arrived from Mong Mao, a Kingdom at the borders of Burma and Yunnan in China, to eastablish the **Ahom** kingdom.The Ahom Kings eventually unified the region into the Ahom Kingdom, which ruled Assam for over 600 years.

The Ahoms, had state recorders who wrote a gazette, called **Burunji** . All events thereafter have been written and are the basis of the modern history of Assam

In the late 18th. Century the Ahom Kingdom started to decline, due to the Maomoria rebellion, protesting the land ownership laws. The Burmese kings, taking advantage of the situatio invaded Assam in early 19th century. It is probably the darkest period of Assamese history. The people were terrorized and eventually the British marched in at the behest of the local king .The British defeated the Burmese and the Yandaboo Treaty was signed.

This was the beginning of the period of British rule.

17th century

1602
The Nawab of Dhaka attacks Lakshmi Narayana of Koch Hajo, the beginning of Mughal interest.

1609
Momai Tamuli Borbarua restructures Paik system in Ahom kingdom.

1662
Mir Jumla occupies Garhgaon, the Ahom capital.

1663
After Treaty of Ghilajharighat Mir Jumla returns to Dhaka, dies on the way.

1671
Ahoms wins Battle of Saraighat

1679
Laluk-sola Borphukan deserts Guwahati

1681
Gadadhar Singha becomes Ahom swargadeo

1682
Ahoms win battle at Itakhuli.
Mughals do not try to retake Koch Hajo again.

assam, the Golden Valley

18th century

1769
First phase of Moamoria rebellion, Ahom capital falls but recaptured in few months

1783
Ahom capital Rangpur fell the second time to Moamoria rebellion. Rebel leaders strike coins in their names.

1794
Captain Thomas Welsh restores Rangpur to Ahom king from Moamora rebels.

19th century

1817
The first Burmese invasion of Assam

1826
Treaty of Yandaboo signed between the East India Company and the Burmese.

assam, the Golden Valley

Colonial Assam

Thereafter the systematic annexation of Assam was pursued by the British between 1824 and completed in 1839

1826-1873

With the successful manufacture of Tea in 1837 it became imperative to include Assam, initially as a part of Bengal Presidency administratively.

1874-1905

Sylhet was added to Assam and a separate, independent Chief Commissioner's Province was formed.

1905-1912

Bengal was partitioned and the East Bengal was added to the Assam Chief Commissioner's office with headquarters at Dacca. This was directly ruled by a Lt. Governer. During the period migration from East Bengal was encouraged in order to enhance the rice production in the valley. This migration is continuing to date.

1912-1920

The Assam Legislative Council was formed.

Ancient Monuments in Assam

Monument	Place	District
Cachari Ruins	Khaspur	Cachar
Dwelling houses		
Baradwari		
East Wall		
Singh Darwaza		
Shan Mandir		
Temples		
Idgah, Mosque.	Rangamati Hill	Dhubri
Surya Pahar Ruins	Dasabhuja	Goalpara
Ancient Tombs	Jogighopa	Nowgong
Monolithe	Kasomari Pahar	Golaghat
Sivadol	Negriting	Golaghat
Carvings at Urvasi Island	Guwahati	Kamrup
Rockcut Sculptures of Vishnu/Surya/Ganesh	Guwahati	Kamrup
Poa Mecca Mosque Inscription	Hajo	Kamrup
Duargarilla Rock Inscriptions	Kamakhya	Kamrup
Dancing Bhairava	Kamakhya	Kamrup
Ganesh		
Narkasur		
4 handed Bhairawa		
Sikhara Shrine		
Siva Lingas		
Stone gateway		
2 handed Bhairava		
Sri Kedar Temple	Hajo	Kamrup
Ancient Ganesh Temple	Hajo	Kamrup
Ancient Remains of Kameshwar Temple	Hajo	Kamrup
Cachari Ruins	Khaspur	Cachar
Dwelling houses		
Baradwari		
East Wall		
Singh Darwaza		
Shan Mandir		
Temples		
Idgah, Mosque.	Rangamati Hill	Dhubri
Surya Pahar Ruins	Dasabhuja	Goalpara
Ancient Tombs	Jogighopa	Nowgong
Monolithe	Kasomari Pahar	Golaghat
Sivadol	Negriting	Golaghat
Carvings at Urvasi Island	Guwahati	Kamrup
Rockcut Sculptures of Vishnu/Surya/Ganesh	Guwahati	Kamrup
Poa Mecca Mosque Inscription	Hajo	Kamrup
Duargarilla Rock Inscriptions	Kamakhya	Kamrup

Dancing Bhairava	Kamakhya	Kamrup
Ganesh		
Narkasur		
4 handed Bhairawa		
Sikhara Shrine		
Siva Lingas		
Stone gateway		
2 handed Bhairava		
Sri Kedar Temple	Hajo	Kamrup
Ancient Ganesh Temple	Hajo	Kamrup
Ancient Remains of Kameshwar Temple	Hajo	Kamrup
Rockcut Kachari Temple	Maibong	Cachar
Ancient inscribed stones		
Boloson Group Monoliths	North Cachar	Cachar
Derebara Group Monoliths	North Cachar	Cachar
Khartong Group Monoliths	North Cachar	Cachar
Kobak Group Monoliths	North Cachar	Cachar
Four Maidams, Burial grounds	Charaideo	Sibsagar
Ahom Palace	Gargaon	Sibsagar
Bishnudol	Gaurisagar	Sibsagar
Devidol		
Sivadol		
Gaurisagar Tank		
Bishnudol	Jaysagar	Sibsagar
Devidol		
Ghanshyam House		
Golaghar		
Karengghar		
Ranghar		
Sivadol		
Rangnathdopl	Meteka	Sibsagar
Bishunudol	Sibsagar	Sibsagar
Devidol		
8 Ahom Cannons		
Sivadol	Sibsagar	Sibsagar
Bordoloi temple	Bishwanath	Sonitpur
Rock known as 'Sakreswar on the Island'.		Sonitpur
Bishwanath SIvaling	Sonitpur	Sonitpur
Dhandi Temple	Nc Hills	Cachar
Ruins	Kamdayal	Sonitpur
Masonary Remains	Bamuni Hills	Sonitpur
Mounds and remains of Stone Temple	Tezpur	Sonitpur
Sculptures of theChummery Compound	Sonitpur	Sonitpur
Hayagriva Temple		

Printed in Great Britain
by Amazon